T0086186

Other Books by James R. Holbrook

Potsdam Mission:
Memoir of a U.S. Army Intelligence Officer in Communist East Germany

Moscow Memoir:
An American Military Attaché in the USSR 1979-1981

Outline of Colloquial/Conversational Russian

Linguistic Overview of the System

James R. Holbrook

Author of two memoirs: Potsdam Mission and Moscow Memoir

OUTLINE OF COLLOQUIAL/CONVERSATIONAL RUSSIAN
LINGUISTIC OVERVIEW OF THE SYSTEM

iUniverse books may be ordered through booksellers or by contacting:

iUniverse
1663 Liberty Drive
Bloomington, IN 47403
www.iuniverse.com
844-349-9409

ISBN: 978-1-6632-4980-7 (sc)
ISBN: 978-1-6632-4979-1 (e)

Library of Congress Control Number: 2023900821

Print information available on the last page.

iUniverse rev. date: 02/09/2023

CONTENTS

AUTHOR'S NOTE

Colloquial Russian is conversational Russian. It has its own system and norms. Educated Russians use CR in everyday speech. Additionally, CR is often found in literature and other print forms, as well as in radio and TV.

The primary purposes of this book are: (1) to highlight the importance of Colloquial Russian in the classroom and (2) to identify the differences between the standard language found in textbooks and the conversational Russian of educated native speakers.

Russian scholars call Standard Russian the Codified Literary Language (*кодифицированный литературный язык*), abbreviated in Russian as *КЛЯ.* Colloquial Russian is *русская разговорная речь,* abbreviated in Russian as *РРР* (or *разговорный язык*, abbreviated РЯ). I use the abbreviations KLJ for codified and CR for colloquial Russian in this book.

When I first began to study CR in the early 1970s, I found that B. Unbegauen's 1950 article "Colloquial and Literary Russian" did not, in fact, deal with the structure of modern colloquial speech. Instead, the article covered the history of the influence of Church Slavonic, French and spoken Russian on the development of literary Russian.

As far as I could determine, there were no English-language materials on CR available in the United States, not even in the Library of Congress.[1] I seized upon a footnote in a Russian article that revealed a book on CR had been published at Saratov University in the USSR. I then fired off five letters to Soviet organizations I thought might be able to help me acquire that book.

Finally, in 1974, I received the book—*Русская разговорная речь* (RRR-70)—published in only 2000 copies.[2] Additionally, the authors sent me E.A. Zemskaya's 1973 *Русская разговорная речь*, referred to throughout this book as RRR-73. RRR-73 turned out to be the seminal volume in the study of CR. Almost all CR scholars cite this book in their work; E.A. Zemskaya even cites it in her later work. The main value of RRR-73 and later treatments of CR in Russia is that almost all examples are based on live, recorded samples of modern CR authenticated by Russian scholars. I collected no samples outside the USSR/Russia.

I used those books as the basis for the treatment of CR in my doctoral dissertation at Georgetown University. What drew me to this subject was that during my teaching Russian at the West Point Military Academy, cadets would come to me expressing their lack of comprehension when reading Soviet literature even though they understood all the words.[3]

After Georgetown, my Army duties, including a tour at the U.S. Embassy in Moscow, prevented me from pursuing academic work on CR. Ironically, while serving in Moscow in the late 1970s and early 1980s, each time I visited the central, open-air swimming pool, I passed the Soviet Academy's Institute of the Russian Language where Zemskaya was working inside. Due to my status as a member of the Embassy staff, I deemed it inappropriate to contact her or her colleagues at the Institute because it might cause them political difficulties.

A few years later, after retirement from the army and intelligence work, I did get to visit Zemskaya during another sojourn in Moscow (1994-96), when I headed a joint US-Russian translation project for chemical demilitarization.

Happily, the dearth of work on CR in the United States that I faced in the early 1970s has been somewhat ameliorated. There are now some research materials available. In particular, the collection *Topics in Colloquial Russian* (1990), edited by Margaret Mills, contains valuable articles on the linguistics and classroom presentation of CR. She treated colloquial word order in her PhD dissertation at the University of Michigan in 1985. Word order was also the topic for Asya Pereltsvaig in *Studia Linguistica*, 2008.

An excellent newer addition to the study of CR is Mark T. Hooker's *Implied But Not Stated: Condensation in Colloquial Russian* (2006). In 2014, the first of a possible five-volume dictionary of CR words was published in Moscow: L. P. Krysin's *Толковый словарь русской разговорной* речи. In 2016, V.K. Kharchenko's published a five-volume *Антология русской разговорной речи.* Those books and later articles in such publications as *Русский язык за рубежом, Russian Language Journal, Русский язык в национальной школе* and *Slavic and East European Journal* have made it possible for me to catch up on the work done on CR since my Georgetown days. Worldcat.com and scholar.google.com yielded several books and articles under the keyword "Colloquial Russian," but most of them dealt with words and phrases called "colloquialisms." Even in textbooks titled Colloquial Russian, the term "colloquialism" is widespread. Nowhere in English is there a treatment of CR as a system with its own norms.

As chaotic as CR might first appear, it has a system of its own—one whose structures can be identified and some of which can be applied to the teaching of Russian. Hopefully, a presentation of these systematic aspects of CR will facilitate overcoming the disadvantage students now face in most Russian language programs. This book is intended for teachers, textbook authors and program designers—although students, other scholars and practitioners of the Russian language may also find the information useful.

Thus, this is not an original linguistics book. It's a review and presentation of much of the work that Soviet/Russian (and some Western) scholars have done. Most of the information herein (with few exceptions) is derivative, as it must be, since almost all the examples and much of the analysis is taken from the work of Soviet/Russian scholars. Although many of the examples are old, sometimes by decades, the patterns shown here remain valid in contemporary CR. The colloquial examples taken directly from Soviet/Russian sources are presented here in bold.[4] To minimize the number of endnotes, sources for those examples are in parentheses.

The book defines CR and its place in the overall Russian language. Separate chapters present characteristics of colloquial phonetics, morphology, syntax, word order and vocabulary. Finally, a chapter of recommendations may be useful to textbook writers or teachers who wish to introduce aspects of CR into the Russian language classroom.

CHAPTER 1

Why Did She Say That?

Picture this: You're a graduate of a good Russian program and find yourself on a bus in Moscow, going up Tverskaya Street. The bus stops and a Russian woman behind you says:

> **Маяковка. Сходите?**
> (Кост 1965:15)

Why did she say that? What did she mean? You didn't understand. But weren't you an 'A' student when you majored in Russian at the university? At the time, you considered yourself to be fluent in the language. You look at the Russian woman with dismay. By this time, the woman is getting a bit impatient. You notice people are getting off the bus. Oh! She probably wants to get off and you're standing in her way.

Later, as you reflect on this episode, you might think—based on the Russian you learned at the university—the Muscovite wasn't speaking 'proper' Russian. If the woman had wanted you to move so she could get off, why didn't she say: *Вы выходите на Площади Маяковского? Разрешите пройти.* Little might you know that, according to V.G. Kostomarov, under the circumstances, the second utterance would have been a bit pretentious or affected to a native speaker of Russian.

What you encountered on that bus was Colloquial Russian. It was not incorrect Russian. It's the way educated Russians speak in unrehearsed, informal situations.

The above scenario would be an example of what Kostomarov described in the journal *Русский язык в национальной школе*:

> It is well known that foreign students of Russian abroad are absolutely helpless in the everyday communications situation. The fact of the matter is that they have been taught the bookish style (in the written and even lately in the spoken form) but have no training in the colloquial style. This unnatural, bookish language in ordinary situations surprises their Russian listeners.[5]

Zemskaya writes that "Every fluent speaker of Russian senses when someone violates the norms [of colloquial Russian]." She gives this example:

Он человек ужасный / говорит книжный языком / даже картошку картофелем называет //
(Зем 1987:17)

He's a terrible person. He uses bookish language, even calls a a potato by its old German name.

E.A. Klochkova writes that "In our speech we never use such utterances as:

Пошла в театр имени Вахтангова, имени Горького,
I went to the theater named for Vakhtangov or named for Gorky,
но всегда говорим пошла в Вахтанговский, в Горьковский."
but rather we say to the Vakhtangov or the Gorky."
(Клочк 1970:128)

Kostomarov, one of the pioneer scholars of contemporary CR, traveled to England where he met many students of Russian. When he returned, he stated: "Students in England speak an unacceptable bookish language."[6]

The matter of understanding direct, live speech could be greatly simplified, if you were to inform your interlocutor that you're a foreigner. From that point on, the conversation or instructions would probably be conducted in a way more similar to that found in your college textbook. You would have no control, however, over the speech used on radio and TV, in the movies or in newspapers. Comprehension of CR, in both the oral and written forms, is perhaps the most important and difficult task for the student.

Kostomarov provides a couple of examples that illustrate not only the contrast between KLJ and CR, but also the wide variety of response patterns to a simple question in CR. For example, in answer to the completely innocuous question ***Где ты был?*** we might expect ***Я был дома*** or simply ***Дома.*** Kostomarov states, however, that "an elementary observation of speech shows that this is not the case... In colloquial speech there is no such 'plain' communication. Normal, natural conversation could not be carried out without some emotional or expressive devices." In reality, according to him, the most likely CR answer to this question would be one of the following:

Да дома!
Где – дома.
Да где я был – дома.
Где ж мне быть – дома.
Я – дома.
Я-то? – Да дома.
Где был-то? – Да дома.
(Кост 1966:64.)

This illustrates one of the complex aspects of CR; there is no single response to many questions. The student needs a wide variety of responses in order to assimilate some of the patterns in CR. Fortunately, as we will see in this book, not all problems associated with colloquial speech are formidable.

A critical skill for students is the reading of literature. CR appears in some classics, but primarily in modern Russian literature. The editors of a reader of contemporary literature wrote in their introduction:

> For the student of Russian, this anthology provides a good sample of the contemporary colloquial language. The student can rightly complain of the rigid diet of nineteenth century reading that is prescribed for him.[7]

One of the chief reasons for this, according to those editors is:

> …the strong disapproval of the great changes in the Russian language that have occurred in the past few decades… The American student has been carefully shielded from these linguistic facts of life, on the premise that he should learn the 'pure' Russian of pre-revolutionary times.

N. Isotov, in his review of V. Nekrasov's "Kira Georgievna" wrote:

> One encounters many words and expressions quite unfamiliar to an ear, which has been out of touch with Soviet reality... The language of Kira Georgievna is not an isolated phenomenon... These words and expressions seem to be well established and not unfamiliar to the educated ear in the Soviet Union... It is evident that to teach modern Russian by way of Pushkin, Lermontov and Turgenev is to be blind to the present and to deprive the student of the spoken word.[8]

Ronald Hingley, noting the difficulty students have with contemporary Russian literature, wrote in 1959:

> ...the greatest difficulty of all lies in the extraordinarily wide vocabulary used by Soviet authors, ... and constructions often ignored in the most comprehensive dictionaries and grammars. .... One cannot read much of their work without a thorough grasp of the modern colloquial idiom such as no hitherto study aid aims to give.[9]

More recently (2008), Krysin pointed out:

> In the last two decades, the role of oral-colloquial speech has grown significantly. Colloquial and popular speech, jargon and syntax that are characteristic of oral discourse is now a common phenomenon not only in everyday communication, but also in the public sphere and the media. The movement of 'colloquialness' into those spheres began, it appears, at a time when politicians stopped reading their speeches and various oral interviews involved more or less spontaneous conversation. Talk shows and other forms of unrehearsed communication started appearing in the electronic media, on radio and TV. Linguists write of the unprecedented and uncharacteristic colloquialization (that is, the plethora of colloquial elements) that had never occurred earlier in Russian public communications.[10]

Obviously, all languages change over time; all languages reflect the culture in which they are spoken. It's important, however, that CR as presented here is current and often used in contemporary Russian literature. That fact alone should be sufficient reason to interest teachers in CR. CR is very important in literature not only to the understanding of the plot and the dialogue, but also for a genuine appreciation of the expressive nuances used by an author—one of the primary purposes, after all, of reading foreign literature in the original.

One example of what one may find is shown below, taken from Soviet/Russian literature, illustrating the replacement of *почему* with *что* or *чего*:

- **Вы завтракали? – спросил он.**
- **Завтракал.**
- **Жаль.**
- **А что?**
- **Чего это ты вдруг?**

  (Некрас 1966:109-110)[11]
  - Have you had breakfast? he asked.
  - Yes.
  - Too bad.
  - Why?
  - Why'd you do that all of a sudden?

A simple analysis will show that *что* and *чего* are words that may be substituted for *почему*. To check the validity of this analysis, here are several examples in which *что* and *чего* are used instead of *почему*:

- **Ты что-то плохо выглядишь сегодня.**
- **Возраст такой – ответил Николай Иванович, вставая. Всю ночь чего-то ворочался. И сны всякие дурацкие.**

  (Некрас 1966:94)
  - For some reason or other you look bad today.
  - It's my age, answered Nikolai Ivanovich, getting up. All night I tossed and turned for some reason or other. And I had all kinds of crazy dreams.

- **Ты работаешь сегодня?**
- **Работаю. А что?**
  - Are you working today?
  - Yes. Why do you ask?

  (Некрас 1966:94)

Чёй-то ты в коридоре стал разбуваться?
(Крив 1974:75)

Why did you start taking your shoes off in the corridor?

Что это конфет шоколадных нигде нету?
Лап 1976:210

Why is it there're no chocolate candies anywhere?

Что-то я давно не вижу из нашего дома //
Зем 1973:236

For some reason or other, it's been a long time since I've seen [anyone] from our building.

In the first examples, one sees that *почему-то* could be substituted for both *что-то* and *чего-то*. In the third example, *чёй-то* derives from *чего-это* which, in turn, derives from *почему это*. The addition of *это* is also colloquial, so that the 'original/KLJ' neutral utterance would be: *Почему ты в коридоре*... A similar explanation applies to the last examples.

Further research would show that, indeed, the substitution of *что* and *чего* for *почему* is common in CR (also in the pre-Soviet period.)[12] It would seem, then, that this characteristic of CR could easily be presented to the student of Russian. In fact, however, few popular American textbooks do so. A couple of rare examples are:

А что это вы так идете?
Dawson, 1964:61)[13]

Why are you walking like that?

Что ты стоишь? Снимай куртку и садись.
(*A-LM Level One* 1963:43)

Why you just standing there? Take your jacket off and sit down.
(Perhaps a better translation, one that is more literal but still acceptable in English, might be "What are you standing there for?")

Another important and very common feature of CR is 'deletion.' An example is in the expression *может быть* where the last element *быть* is often deleted:

А <u>может</u> / и совсем молчать //
(Некрас 1971:94)
And maybe [I/you] should be completely quiet.

Хоть ты / Люба / <u>может</u> / покушаешь //
(Фом 1970:6)
At least you, Lyuba, perhaps will have something to eat.

<u>Может</u> / вам что будет нужно / заходите пожалуйста // (Убог 1974)[14]
It may be that you'll need something. If so, drop by.

Here both the full and the abbreviated forms are used together:

<u>Может быть</u>, она думает, что я заговорю, скажу что-нибудь веселое, <u>может</u>, она ждет первого моего слова, вопроса какого-нибудь.
Maybe she thinks I will start talking, that I will say something funny. Maybe she's waiting for me to say something first, like some kind of question. (Каз in Harper et al. 1966:9).

CR frequently uses 'addition' of an element not found in KLJ. The addition of a pronoun to a clause that already has a noun subject is one example where CR parallels colloquial English:

Жизнь / она на месте не стоит //
(Буб 1974:72
Life, it doesn't stand still.

The above examples are taken from dialogue in contemporary Russian literature. Dialogue, both literary and live, is the most common but not the only type of speech in which the student may encounter CR. More and more, Russian authors are using elements of CR in their descriptive and narrative speech. F. Abramov writes that:

> There is a process in modern literature that linguists would do well to note: the boundary between the speech of the characters in a literary work and the speech of the author is not so clear as it was in literature of the XIX century.[15]

A. Krivonosov, for example, 'substitutes' the colloquial diminutive adverbs *чуточку* and *ладненько* and the colloquial particle – *то* in this narrative:

> **...новые сапоги чуточку стискивали пальцы, но, в общем-то, сидели ладненько, даже поскрипывали.** (Крив 1970:37)
>
> ...the new boots squeezed my toes some, but generally they felt ok, even squeaked a bit.

As stated above, the presentation of material in this book hopes to assist the textbook author and teacher in the Russian language classroom. The question of what elements of CR can or should be presented to the student, or how that may be done, should be left to the primary actors—teachers in the classroom. This issue is addressed in the final chapter.

Comprehension of CR—one of the most important skills in learning Russian—would eliminate many frustrations for the student when he or she is reading Russian literature or the press, watching Russian movies or listening to Russian language broadcasts. These activities may occur even outside of Russia—at Russian language club functions, theaters, on CDs that accompany some textbooks, or in language laboratories and classrooms.

More detailed linguistic peculiarities of CR are presented in the following chapters and are oriented primarily toward those characteristics that play an important role in the understanding of CR.

For example, in phonetics the vowel and consonant reductions that occur in speech (spoken CR is almost always rapid in a student's view) are so significant that failure to prepare, to 'warn,' the student may cause him or her to have a complete lack of comprehension when listening to live Russian. Rate of speech, however, is only one contributing factor to these reductions. Many reductions often follow a pattern that is evident in some slower CR utterances.

Morphology does not present such serious problems, but there are significant morphologic changes in CR words that the student should be made aware of.

Syntax and word order in CR, however, due to their close relationship with the situation, intonation and the use of ellipsis, may cause considerable difficulty for the unprepared student. Because of this and the wealth of available variations peculiar to CR, the treatment here of syntax and word order will be quite extensive.

Vocabulary is a particularly dynamic element of speech. A familiarity with several words, phrases and patterns in colloquial vocabulary is critical for the student who wants to understand modern Russian.

CHAPTER 2

Definitions and Sources

DEFINITIONS

What is this Colloquial Russian that the student for the most part is missing in the classroom?

It's imperative that the terms used throughout this book be defined and understood. One of the most prevalent sources of difficulty in gaining acceptance of Colloquial Russian in the classroom is a lack of understanding the term. A Worldcat.com and Scholargoogle.com search of CR revealed numerous websites purporting to be about CR, but listed only Russian idioms or slang.[16] This is not, as we will state several times in this book, Colloquial Russian—the conversational language of educated Russians. Such terms as 'idiomatic Russian' and 'colloquialisms' only obscure the fact that what we are dealing with in CR is a *system* with its own patterns and norms.

First of all, we must admit that there is no all-encompassing definition of CR, since it is so varied and multilayered. V. Khimik provides perhaps the best effort to address its flexibility, levels and overall place in the Russian language in his paper at the 43rd International Philological Conference in St. Petersburg. He is aware of all the Soviet/Russian scholars (e.g., Zemskaya, Lapteva, Krysin et al.) and their definitions of CR, but approaches the subject on a wider, socio-linguistic basis.[17]

Our definition, however, is much simpler and is meant to show only the outlines of CR. It follows the line taken by these latter scholars and coincides with the actual recorded speech presented in our sources.

Perhaps the most comprehensive definition of colloquial speech in general, and one that supports the point of view in this book, is found in *Webster's New International Dictionary*:

> Colloquial—Pertaining to, or used in, conversation, esp. common and familiar conversation; conversational; *hence, unstudied* [italics mine-jrh], informal… acceptable and appropriate in ordinary conversation content, as in intimate speech among cultivated people… *Colloquial speech may be as correct as formal speech.*[18] [italics mine-jrh]

We will use Zemskaya's definition of CR as: "Unprepared speech of educated Russians under the conditions of direct, unofficial discourse."[19] She also points out that CR has its own system of norms. Likewise, N.Yu. Shvedova wrote:

> It is usually thought that colloquial speech is more freely constructed than written speech. That it does not have its own strict norms and formulas… However, this freedom is in many ways misleading… a result of the weak study of the immense amount of appropriate material… *Oral speech has organized forms of its construction.*[20] [Italics mine jrh)

The significance of CR norms, when compared to those of the codified language, led over the years to a lively discussion among Soviet/Russian scholars over what to call CR. Was it a style or a language?

Since CR performs the communication function better than any other version of Russian in everyday conversation, it was originally referred to by many writers as a 'functional style' *(функциональный стиль).* Together with other functional styles, such as newspaper, official, radio-TV, belles-lettres and scientific, it comprised an integral part of the Russian language. This was the view originally held by several Soviet/Russian scholars. The question of style in languages has held a long-term interest among linguists. O.S. Lapteva lists over forty works devoted to style.[21]

In 1973, Zemskaya rejected the term 'functional style.'[22] For some time after that, she referred to CR as a variant (*разновидность*) of the language. She apparently wanted to call CR a separate language, but continued to use the term *разговорная речь*. She explained that out of tradition, she was still using that term to refer to CR. Nonetheless, she argued, the subject of investigation was more than a functional style.

Her argument was summed up as follows:

CR so differs from KLJ that it cannot be viewed simply as a style of the language. For example, some of the peculiarities of CR, which are not present in KLJ are:

(1) the situation or 'situational context' (*конситуация)* is a full-fledged constituent of the conversation;

(2) gestures enter into CR to such an extent that they often duplicate or even replace linguistic elements;

(3) intonation plays an especially important role in CR;

(4) non-canonical phonetics is important in CR; and

(5) the unidirectional nature of the speech stream, i.e., the impossibility of returning to the starting point of speech.[23]

Originally, this author felt these factors appeared to be insufficient to remove the label 'functional style' from CR. To one extent or another points (2), (3) and (5) are present in other functional styles when found in the spoken form. Zemskaya herself noted that gestures (point 2) are absent in telephone conversations. We should add that this applies also to personal letters in which CR is the most common version of the language.

The study of CR became more detailed and revealed a multitude of systemic variations from KLJ, most of which did not apply to the functional styles noted above. Thus, we can now accept Zemskaya's definition. Essentially, the CR system is unique at all levels—phonology, morphology, syntax, word order and vocabulary. As Zemskaya points out, not only does CR differ in the selection of items, but many of these items function differently from KLJ.[24]

The extra-linguistic situation (point 1) plays an extremely important role in the selection of items, especially in spoken CR. Among these extra-linguistic factors are the following: the discourse is unofficial, direct, allows for participation of all speakers; differs according to whether it is oral or written; depends on the situation; uses gestures; and depends on whether it is dialogue, monologue or polylogue.[25]

Zemskaya argues that CR and KLJ can be likened to the chess game that de Saussure described. Namely, although all the pieces belong to the same game, the rules (systemic functions) are different. In the two variants of Russian, not only is the number of pieces (linguistic units) different, but many pieces common to both CR and KLJ behave differently within their respective systems. By 2014, Zemskaya explained:

> The observant reader will immediately note that we characterize the object of our research as colloquial **language**. [Emphasis Zemskaya] In [earlier] work when we viewed this subject, we called it colloquial **speech**. [Emphasis Zemskaya] We did that for a long time, not wishing to disavow the long-time tradition of colloquial speech in Russian studies… In publications of the last decades, the term colloquial language has been used (cf. French - *Français parle,* German - *Umgangssprache,* Czech - *Hovorová čestina* and similar names in other languages).[26]

The current term by Zemskaya is now *литературный разговорный язык*, 'literary conversational language.' She uses the abbreviation РЯ (*разговорный язык*). 'Literary' here is not to be confused with 'literary Russian' in the English sense—*язык художественной литературы*—which is referred to in this book as the style of belles-lettres. 'Literary' in the sense Zemskaya uses it simply means the language of educated Russians.

In his longitudinal study of Russian syntax, M.V. Panov points out that "the colloquial style in the XIX-XX centuries developed into an independent form of intercourse" and "Colloquial Russian in its oral manifestation became a special, independent form of speech."[27]

In fact, for our purposes, it is not really so important what the Russian scholars call Colloquial Russian. Our purpose is simply to describe this conversational language as evidenced by our examples. So we repeat: Colloquial Russian is not slang or sloppy speech. It is the conversational Russian of educated native speakers and has norms of its own. Our use of the abbreviation CR remains the same: Colloquial Russian.

The term 'utterance' (*высказывание)* is used here to denote a unit of speech roughly analogous to a sentence. Although this distinction may seem contrived, the deviations in CR from KLJ sentences make this term more accurate and convenient. We are looking at utterances that actually exist in speech, fixed by sound recordings and transcription.

The next definition deals with the term 'form.' Here form denotes the manner in which the language is made manifest. For the purposes of this book, there are two forms: written and spoken. CR occurs most often in the spoken form, but often is also written.[28] It's important to remember that CR takes place when the appropriate conditions are met. In spoken form the speech is unrehearsed (*неподготовленная*), relaxed *(непринужденная)* and usually direct (*непосредственное общение*). The written form is intended to replicate or assume those conditions exist to the extent possible. For example, written CR is found in personal notes or letters and in literary dialogue, which is to be perceived as speech in the spoken form.

The spoken form, on the other hand, is not the exclusive domain of CR. Lectures, radio and TV broadcasts, as well as speeches at public gatherings are in the spoken form, but need not be in CR.

Because some people confuse CR with such terms as 'spoken language', 'dialogue' and 'monologue' speech, it's also necessary to define those terms used in this book. These are 'types' of speech. 'Type' is related to the number of speakers involved in a conversation. Monologue and dialogue are types, although they may be in written or spoken form. CR occurs also in polylogue. Both the form and type of speech influence the choice of linguistic elements available to the speaker or writer. That choice is also dependent on other, extra-linguistic, factors, some of which have already been mentioned. They include subject matter, age and education of the speaker or writer, the attitude of the speaker toward the subject matter and toward his listener. (See the standards by which informants were selected by Soviet/Russian scholars discussed below.)

These, then, are the definitions of the major concepts that underlie the presentation of CR in this book. Most important for the reader, however, is to realize that we're not talking about slang, jargon or substandard speech.

SOURCES

Research into CR history and its study took place in Russian sources.[29]

What is the nature of the source material used by Soviet/Russian scholars and represented in this book? Accuracy and reliability of data in any field of research is directly related to the technical means of collecting and identifying that data.

It is understandable that early studies of CR relied heavily on less-than-ideal sources. Specifically, the 1960 study by Shvedova (*Очерки по синтаксису русской разговорной речи*) relied mainly on dialogue in belles-lettres. She clearly recognized this somewhat limiting factor and comments on it extensively in her book. So, in addition to literary dialogue, she used hand-written transcription of live speech "heard in the family, at work, on the train, on the street, etc."[30] Using examples from Shvedova is justified if we accept her statement that the most salient peculiarities of CR can be obtained from belles-lettres. She writes:

> ...material extracted from [good] belles-lettres, especially from the works of masters of Russian realistic prose, may serve as a reliable source for the

> study of the main lexical-grammatical forms of the diverse constructions that are characteristic of Russian colloquial speech.[31]

T. G. Vinokur supported this argument:

> ...dialogues and monologues of [literary] personages contain the quintessence of the typical features of colloquial speech... For that very reason, belles-lettres is a reliable source for the study of colloquial speech, together with recordings of live speech.[32]

Others believed, and to a certain extent demonstrated, that literary dialogue and live speech differ significantly. A. P. Zhuralev, upon investigating various elements of dialogue in prose, dialogue in drama and live speech, concludes that "colloquial speech in belles-lettres is not a copy of live speech, although the speech represented in drama is closer to it than the dialogue in prose."[33] Still, since one of the first contacts the student will have with colloquial speech may be in literature and other printed sources, Shvedova's examples are appropriate in this book.

The overwhelming majority of the published research on CR since the mid-1960s, however, has been based on the tape recording (and some hand transcription) of live speech. The current source for many of these studies is a tape library at the Academy of Sciences in Moscow. This effort was begun in 1963 and by 1967 over 64,000 meters of tape had been recorded. Taping had been going on elsewhere, but it appears the Academy is the central repository and clearing house for most of these efforts. Zemskaya reports that by 1973, the Academy was in possession of 325 hours of recorded colloquial speech from Moscow and Leningrad alone. This material is classified according to three types of speech: monologue, dialogue and polylogue, and according to whether it was recorded in Moscow or Leningrad.[34]

The next question concerns the description of informants from whom the material was collected. Zemskaya (RRR-73) provides the most detailed description of these informants. Keeping in mind that the method used was to record the speech of educated native speakers under appropriate colloquial conditions, Zemskaya used the following three criteria to define the 'educated native speaker:'

(1) Russian was the native language;

(2) the informant was born and reared in the city (and thus, as a rule did not use dialect traits in speech); and

(3) the informant had at least a 'middle' and in most cases a 'higher' education.

These criteria alone, it was felt, should drastically reduce dialectal or non-standard speech. In cases of doubt, however, a 'collective' evaluation was made, eliminating an element if at least one of five investigators would not accept it in standard CR.[35]

The actual informants, on whose speech RRR-73 was based, were natives of Moscow or Leningrad. They were divided into three age groups—17-27 years, 28-49 years and 50 years or older. By profession they were manual laborers (middle education), engineers, chemists, physicists, geologists, doctors, art scholars, historians, high-school and college teachers, librarians, bookkeepers, translators, linguists, artists, metallurgists, a violinist, an actor, a writer and a ballerina. These informants were selected in order to reduce or eliminate regional dialects (*местные говоры*) and sub-standard Russian (*просторечие*). Some of those last two elements, however, do appear in live speech and may be included in the examples cited in this book.[36]

The following extra-linguistic information was also considered for the informants:

(1) year of birth
(2) place of birth
(3) place of longest stay
(4) profession
(5) knowledge of foreign languages
(6) profession and education of parents
(7) parents' birthplace

In defining the presence of the 'appropriate colloquial conditions,' the following three criteria were used:

(1) spontaneity of speech
(2) casualness of speech
(3) direct participation in the conversation

Every effort was made to establish these conditions, even though the quality of a recording might suffer due to interfering noise, such as dishes, furniture being moved, etc.[37]

Identification of as many extra-linguistic factors as possible is of no small importance, since each has, to a greater or lesser degree, some impact on the linguistic peculiarities of CR. Among additional factors felt to be important by Zemskaya were:

(1) form of speech (spoken or written)
(2) number of speakers
(3) contact versus distance of speakers (an example of the latter would be a telephone conversation)
(4) the presence or absence of the object of speech.

Other more psycholinguistic factors also determine certain linguistic characteristics of CR. For example, the speaker-hearer's attitude toward the object of conversation, his or her attitude toward and familiarity with the other participants and whether the utterances are interrogative, declarative, affective or motivative (*побудительные*).[38]

CHAPTER 3

Brief History of the Use and Study of Colloquial Russian

USE OF COLLOQUIAL RUSSIAN

It is, of course, impossible to arrive at any definitive picture of early colloquial speech in Russia. Nonetheless, many studies devoted to the history of the Russian language reveal interesting information. (Unbegauen's article is pertinent here.)

In early Kievan Russia, before the advent of writing, live speech was the only speech (as in any society). As Old Church Slavonic (OCS) became more prominent, it appears the differences between live speech and OCS were at first insignificant. For example, in the *Primary Chronicle* (898), the following passage appears:

> **Бе един язык словенеск... А словеньский язык и рускый одно есть...**
> (Горш 1969:39)[39]
>
> There was one Slavonic language... The Slavonic language and Russian are the same.

I.I. Sreznevsky viewed OCS and Russian of the Kievan period as simply representing different styles (*слоги*) of the same language, with OCS differing "very little from the speech of the people."[40] Nonetheless, there are some examples of 'literary dialogue' in which, presumably, there is an attempt to portray the actual speech of individuals. In the *Primary Chronicle's* account of the blinding of Vasilko, for example, one reads:

> **и рече Василко не могу остати брате. уже есмь повелѣл товаром поити переди… и рече Святополкъ посѣдита вы сдѣ. А язь лѣзу наряжю…**
> (Улух 1972:95)[41]
>
> And Vasilko said: "I cannot stay brother. I've already ordered my camp to move forward…" And Sviatapolk said: "Remain seated here a moment while I go out…"

One of the best sources for examples of colloquial Russian during the early Moscow period is the *Travels of Afanasy Nikitin (*or *The Journey Beyond Three Seas* (1466-72)). A. Gorshkov suggests that colloquial Russian actually dominates in this work. Note, for example, the nomination phenomenon common to modern CR (discussed below in the Vocabulary chapter) in the last phrase of this passage:

> **И мы поехали к Ширванше во Коитул и били есмя ему челом, чтобы нас пожаловал <u>чем доити до Руси</u>…**
> (Горш 1969:113)[42] [Underscore mine]
>
> And we went to Shirvansha and begged him to give us [pay us] something with which we could reach [get back to] Russia…

The following excerpt from Nikitin illustrates a simplicity of syntactic constructions and concrete, but expressive, nature of vocabulary:

> **И есть тут Индийская страна, и люди ходят все голые: голова не покрыта, груды голы, волосы в одну косу плетены. Все ходят брюхаты, детей родят каждый год, и детей у них много. Мужи и жены все черны. Куда бы я не пошел, так за мной людей много – дивятся белому человеку.**
> (*Хрест 1969*:117)
>
> And there is this country, India. People go around naked. Their heads are not covered, their breasts are bare. And they wear their hair in a single braid. Everyone has a big belly. They have a child a year and there are lots of kids. The men and women are all black. Wherever I went, I was followed by a lot of people. Everyone is amazed to see a white person.

But the differences between early colloquial and more formal speech increased, as can be seen in the following examples. In one edition of *The Life of Klopsky* (Novgorod, 15th century), one finds the colloquial:

> **Михайлушко! Бегаю своей отчины, збили меня с великого княжения.**
> (Улух 1972:93)
>
> Mike! I'm running from my homeland. I've been kicked out of the Grand Princedom.

In a later, 16th century, edition this passage is 'upgraded' to OCS:

> **Отче, моли Бога о мне яко да таки восприиму царствия скырьтры: Согнан бо есмь от своей отчины, великого княжения московского!**
> (Улух 1972:93)
>
> Father, pray to God for me since I must accept the kingdom of the Scythians. I've been exiled from my homeland, the Grand Princedom of Muscovy.

The letters (16th century) from Ivan the Terrible to Prince Kurbsky show some of the most remarkable early examples of expressive and highly emotional colloquial speech in Russian writing:

> **Лице же свое пишешь не явити нам до дня страшного суда Божия. Лице же свое драго показуеши! Хто убо желает такова ефиопьска лица видети?**
> (DLIWC Vol. XI-7:61)
>
> You say you won't show your face here until the Day of Judgement. You really value your face! Who would even want to see such an Ethiopian face?

Certainly one of the earliest and most colorful propagandists for the 'elevation' of colloquial speech to a literary level, was the 17th century Archpriest Avvakum. A rebel in all he did, Avvakum was also a prolific writer. His autobiography and letters are full of colloquial, even substandard elements.

Moreover, Avvakum entreated everyone to write and speak that way. In a letter to the Tsar, Avvakum wrote:

> **Ты ведь, Михайлович, русак, а не грек. Говори своим прородным языком. Не уничижай ево и в церкви, и в дому, и в пословицах.** (DLJWC Vol. XI-7:61)
>
> After all, Mikhailovich, you're a Russian not a Greek. Speak in your native language. Don't lower it, neither in church, nor in the home, nor in proverbs.

During the era of Peter the Great, there occurred a major upheaval and secularization of Russian society and the Russian language. In attempting to avoid the use of the 'high' OCS style, colloquial speech became much more widely used in writing. This is attested to by such terms used to denote the desired literary language as *простой русский язык* (plain Russian language), *просторечие* (popular, substandard), *гражданское непосредственное наречие* (citizen direct speech), *обходительный язык* (language of everyday intercourse) and *язык, каковым мы меж собой говорим* (the language we use among ourselves).[43]

Since then, several prominent writers have expressed a preference for what they interpreted as the simpler, colloquial style. A.D. Kantemir (1708-1744) wrote, for example:

> **Обыкши я подло и низким штилем писать…**
> (Горш 1969:192)
>
> I am used to writing meanly and in a low style.

V.K. Trediakovsky (1703-1769) shows a similar attitude in the introduction to one of his translations:

> **На меня, прошу я покорно, не извольте погневаться (буде вы еще глубокословныя держитесь славенщизны), что я оную не славенским языком перевел, но почти самым простым русским словом, то есть каковым мы меж собой говорим. Сие я учинил следующих ради причин. Первая: язык славенской у нас есть язык церковной, а сия книга мирская. Другая: язык славенской в нынешном веке у нас очюнь темен, и многия его наши читая не разумеют, а сия книга есть сладкия любви, того ради всем должна быть вразумительна. Третия: которая вам покажется**

> **может быть самая легкая, но которая у меня идет за самую важную, то есть, что язык славенской ныне жесток моим ушам слышится, хотя прежде сего не только я им писывал, но и разговаривал со всеми: но за то у всех я прошу прощения, при которых я с глупословием моим славенским особым речеточцем хотел себя показывать.** (Горш 1969:194)
>
> I sincerely ask you not to get angry at me (if you are one who still believes in the widespread use of Slavonisms) because I have not done this translation in Slavonic. I have used almost the simplest style, that is, the one with which we talk among ourselves. I have done this for the following reasons: First, the Slavonic language is a church language, and this is a secular book. Secondly, the Slavonic language in our time is to us very dark and many of our readers do not understand it. This is a book of sweet love. Therefore, it should be understood by all. Thirdly—a reason you might consider insignificant, but which to me is the most important—the Slavonic language hurts my ears, although I myself not only have written in it, but have also used it in conversation. For that I also ask forgiveness of all in whose presence I attempted to make myself appear eloquent by the use of high-sounding words.

An interesting variation on the style of speech thought desirable stemmed from a movement led by N.M. Karamzin (1766-1820). Karamzin introduced what he called a "new style" (*новый слог*), the main principle of which was "to write like we speak and speak like we write." The problem was that Karamzin had in mind in his "how we speak" that of 'high' or 'polite' society. In most circles of high or polite society, however, the conversational speech was French! What could Karamzin have had in mind when he articulated the idea above? Apparently, in Russian he was most of all interested in the "speak like we write." This "as we write" would have to be invented by talented writers. In Karamzin's words:

> **Что ж остается делать автору? Выдумывать, сочинять выражения; угадывать лучший выбор слов; давать старым некоторый новый смысл, предлагать их в новой связи, но столь искусно, чтобы обмануть читателей и скрыть их от них необыкновенность выражения!... Французы пишут, как говорят,**

а русские обо многих предметах должны еще говорить так, как напишет человек с талантом.
(Горш 1969:303)

> What does the writer have to do? To think up, compose expressions; to figure out the best choice of words; to add a new sense to old words and propose new arrangements. But so cleverly that the reader is deceived and doesn't see the unusualness of the expression. The French write as they speak, but Russians on many subjects should speak the way a talented person writes.

It's obvious that Karamzin's concept of "how we speak" differed significantly from that of earlier proponents of its use in literature, including Avvakum, Peter 1, Trediakovsky and others. Even A.S. Pushkin acknowledged the importance of recognizing the differences and uses of the spoken and written word. Pushkin wrote:

Разговорный язык простого народа (не читающего иностранных книг и, слава богу, не выражающего, как мы, своих мыслей на французском языке) достоин также глубочайших исследований…не худо нам иногда прислушиваться к московским просвирням. Они говорят удивительно чистым и правильным языком.
(Горш 1969:329)[44]

> The colloquial language of the simple people (who don't read foreign books and, thank God, don't express themselves like us in French) deserves thorough research as well… It wouldn't be a bad idea for us sometimes to listen in on the speech of the Moscow women who bake communion bread. They speak a remarkably pure and correct Russian.

A few years later he writes:

Может ли письменный язык быть совершенно подобным разговорному? Нет, так же, как разговорный язык никогда не может быть совершенно подобным письменному… Письменный язык оживляется поминутно выражениями, рождающимися в разговоре, но не должен отрекаться от приобретенного им в

> **течение веков. Писать единственно языком разговорным – значит не знать языка.**
> (Горш 1969:330)[45]
>
> > Can the written language be just like the colloquial? No, just like the colloquial language cannot be just like the written… The written language is constantly enlivened by expressions arising out of conversation, but it should not completely disassociate itself from its accomplishments over the ages. To write only in the colloquial language means not to know the language.

One can find examples of colloquial speech in the literary dialogue of the great classics of 19th century Russian literature. Indeed, the characterizations of various social and psychological types became, according to G.O. Vinokur, "One of the constant preoccupations of Russian writers."[46] Colloquial usage was often found even in an author's narrative, as in this excerpt from an 1836 article by the literary critic V.G. Belinsky:

> **Но я вижу, что моим «разве» конца не будет. А! Вот в чем дело! Из нашей литературы хотят устроить бальную залу и уже зазывают в нее дам.**
> (Горш 1969:361)[47]
>
> > But I see there'll be no end to my "can it be." Aha! This is what's wrong! They want to make a ballroom out of our literature and are already inviting ladies into it.

EARLY SCHOLARLY INTEREST IN COLLOQUIAL RUSSIAN

The above brief historical account has attempted to illustrate both some examples of early use of CR and some attitudes toward its use during various periods in Russian history. Scholarly interest in the linguistic peculiarities and concomitant extra-linguistic factors began to become evident, however, only during the first part of the 20th century.

A.N. Bogolyubov, for instance, wrote in 1914 that since the difference between writing and speaking was so pronounced, "It is important to understand the difference between these two phenomena and, correspondingly, to alter our approaches to their study."[48] L.P. Yakubinsky, in remarking on the differences between spoken and written speech in a 1923 article on dialogue speech, stated that “written speech is fixed and represents something lasting, somewhat like a piece of literature.”[49] Yakubinsky’s basic premise was that dialogue speech derives many of its linguistic peculiarities from the extra-linguistic factors surrounding the manner in which it manifests itself. In this, he was prescient, as modern scholars of CR do emphasize the importance of extra-linguistic factors. Drawing attention to these factors as the conditions under which dialogue takes place, the aims of the speaker, the visual and intonational accompaniment, he, nevertheless, didn’t specify what the linguistic characteristics of dialogue are.

Several scholars during the 1920s, 1930s and 1940s addressed the question of the impact of the ‘Revolution’ on the development of Russian.[50] The upcoming 50th anniversary of the so-called October Revolution served as a catalyst to the study of the language, which led to research into CR.

A discussion of Russian stylistics, which touched upon CR, took place on the pages of *Вопросы языкознания* in 1954-55. This discussion culminated in a 1955 article by V.V. Vinogradov. Just as Yakubinsky had done earlier, Vinogradov pointed to the extra-linguistic characteristics of dialogue, along with pointing out the richness and expressive potential of intonation variation. Additionally, he quite correctly noted that:

> The structure of dialogue depends very much on the role of colloquial speech, on its relationship to the “literary” language. The nature of this is determined by socio-historical conditions. Moreover, colloquial speech varies qualitatively and functionally at difference periods in the development of a nation.[51]

L.V. Shcherba wrote in 1957 that “You might say that all linguistic changes, which are later established in the standard language are forged and accumulated in the smithy shop of colloquial speech.”[52]

MODERN STUDY OF COLLOQUIAL RUSSIAN

The real linguistic analysis of dialogue and CR, however, may have begun with T.G. Vinokur’s Kandidat dissertation, written in 1953: «О некоторых синтаксических особенностях диалогической речи в современном русском языке».[53] This focus on dialogue continued in several other studies shortly thereafter.[54]

As the parameters of investigation became better defined, it became clear that dialogue was only one manifestation of CR, albeit a major one. Dialogue, for instance, in addition to being the type of speech where CR is most often used, possesses certain other peculiarities—both linguistic and non-linguistic, which are unique to it as a type of speech. Scholars began to focus attention on peculiarities of CR that are independent of the form or type of speech in which they are manifested. D. Shmelev's 1959 article on the use of interrogative pronouns and adverbs in various colloquial structures marked the beginning of a series of articles, which would appear in the 1960s on specific individual peculiarities of CR.[55]

The first attempt to treat a wide range of colloquial syntactic structures is found in Shvedova's pioneering *Очерки...* (referred to above). In addition to a discussion of the general nature of colloquial speech and some widespread misconceptions about it, Shvedova presents a collection, classification and analysis of several hundred examples of colloquial speech taken primarily from belles-lettres, but also some from live speech.

Even after the publication of Shvedova's book, there passed some time before the description of CR began to attract many scholars. Panov wrote in 1962 that CR "is almost completely ignored by linguists."[56] Kostomarov commented in 1965 that CR "is no longer ignored, but still has not become the object of orderly and well-thought-out study..."[57]

It's about this time that serious research and publication on a wide variety of CR issues began to appear. Kostomarov's remarks came in an article, which initiated a two-year discussion on the nature of CR and its role in teaching on the pages of the journal *Русский язык в национальной школе* during 1965-1966. Dealing with syntax and providing valuable examples were Kostomarov, Vinokur, E. Ivanchikova, O. Lapteva and N. Khasanov. In a concluding article, Kostomarov was able to note that all participants in the discussion agreed that:

> ...no longer can live, colloquial speech be ignored... The unjustifiably high prestige of bookishness is decreasing and 'colloquialness' in principle deserves a place in teaching materials.[58]

Certainly, by 1966, interest in CR had increased. In the second issue of *Вопросы языкознания* for 1966, Lapteva published an article dealing with the syntax of CR. In the same year, Shiryaev published an article, "Dialogue Utterances as Sentences," in the journal *Русский язык в школе*. Dialogue was also the subject for an article in *Вопросы языкознания* by A.K. Soloveva, while

Shvedova discussed the influence of CR on the written language—using examples from the press. In issue 1-1967 of *Вопросы языкознания*, Lapteva wrote:

> Scholarly collectives are working on colloquial speech, books are coming out on it and conferences are being held. There are signs that even more people are becoming active in such work, but these are only the first steps. The time has come to evaluate… these efforts.[59]

In this article, Lapteva identified four major problem areas in the study of CR. The first was that of defining the object of investigation. Closely linked with this was the problem of delineating the boundaries and identifying the shared characteristics of CR with dialect and sub-standard speech. Another pertinent problem was that of the nature of the source material (corpus) from which the description of CR could proceed. Thc dialogue in belles-lettres (drama, direct speech in prose works) had served as the source of most studies up to 1967. The consequences of this fact, according to Lapteva, needed to be clarified. Finally, the question of the differences between monologue and dialogue in CR was raised.

In 1967, a new journal on the Russian language began publication: *Русский язык за рубежом*. Many scholars who had been active in CR research shifted their attention to this journal. In fact, two similar articles by T. Vishnyakova on the frequency of adjectives and nouns in CR appeared simultaneously in that journal and *Русский язык в национальной школе*. In 1968, Shiryaev presented an article on verbless predicates.[60] In 1968-1969, A.N. Vasilyeva published a three-part article on constructions in CR using the infinitive, imperative and indicative forms of the verb.[61]

With increasing frequency, results of extensive research began to appear. During the mid-1960s, in various research centers (Moscow, Leningrad, Saratov, etc.) tape recordings were being made of spoken Russian. These were collated with experiments and questionnaires on CR.[62]

The collection RRR-70, referred to above, represented a milestone in the study of CR. Never before had so many topics dealing with CR been presented between two book covers (even gestures are treated). The preface stated "the collection reflects the present state of research on colloquial speech."

In May 1971, Zemskaya published an article in *Вопросы языкознания* in which she summarized the prospectus for the monograph that later became RRR-73. That book turned out to be the bedrock of CR research for several generations. Most of the findings in RRR-73 remain the basis for current assessment of CR.

On the American side, Margaret Mills' *Topics...*(1990) and Mark T. Hooker's *Implied But Not Stated...*(2006) added to the growing research on CR. There has also been some research outside the United States. John Baldwin's *A Formal Analysis of the Intonation...* and Asya Pereltsvaig's "Split phrases in colloquial Russian" in *Studia Linguistica* are two examples. But still there was no work that presented CR as a system separate from KLJ.

A unique dictionary of CR vocabulary began publication in 2014: *Толковый словарь русской разговорной речи.* Edited by Krysin, to date only the first four volumes (of a possible five) have been published. Volume 4 was published in 2021.[63] We deal with this dictionary below in Chapter 8: Vocabulary.

In 2016, a set of books on CR came out that provided material differing in significant ways from all the research that had preceded it: V.K. Kharchenko's *Антология разговорной речи.* This anthology consists of five volumes: covering 8,000 utterances presented in 58 thematic categories.[64] Kharchenko's material is not organized by linguistic structure; instead, she gives a description of the speakers and their situations for each utterance.

CHAPTER 4

Phonetics

Although CR appears also in the written form, it's obvious the natural habitat for colloquial speech is the spoken form. All examples of written CR are attempts to reproduce what is spoken, that is, to convince the reader to perceive what is written as having been actually spoken.

The CR examples in this book are authentic. Russian scholars, writing in various books or journals, provided the examples shown below. As we've noted, the overwhelming majority of these materials is based on tape-recorded and hand-written transcriptions of actual utterances by educated Russians.

Zemskaya points out that there is no one way that a word in CR is pronounced. CR phonetics show great variety. The reductions one encounters may depend on the rate of speech and the habits of the speakers. Obviously, students shouldn't attempt to pronounce all these words in the variations shown below. But they should be apprised, at least, of the fact that the pronunciation of words in CR often differs significantly from KLJ.

PHONETIC NOTATION

In this book we use modified Cyrillic phonetic notation to show the contrast between a word in KLJ and CR.

Brackets [ ] signify that a word or phrase is presented phonetically. Parentheses ( ) indicate a sound may or may not be present. (Brackets are also occasionally used to indicate the adding of a word or phrase in a translation.) Due to the phonetic closeness of the written Russian alphabet to pronunciation, Cyrillic notation should not be too cumbersome. The only phonetic characters that need explanation are the [**Ъ**] (hard sign), which is pronounced [uh] (the English schwa) as in the English word 'but' and [**Ь**] (soft sign), which is a very reduced [**И**]. The simple, single apostrophe [**'**] indicates a palatalized/soft consonant. Where in Russian notation a [**j**] or palatalized consonant precedes [э, a, o, y], we will see [e, я, ё, ю]. For consonants that normally are palatalized, e.g., [**ч**], the vowels remain as they are in the Russian notation. Long consonants in Russian notation are represented here by doubling of the consonant. An asterisk (*) indicates an incorrect pronunciation or word. The following example should assure readers of the ease in using Cyrillic phonetic notation:

Хорошо—[хърашо]—well

As the reader knows, this word in standard orthography has three **O**s. But in colloquial (as well as standard) pronunciation, the **O** and **A** at least two places before stress and all syllables after stress are pronounced [**Ъ**]. The **O** and **A** just preceding stress is an [ah]—indicated here with an [**A**]. A few more examples:

Дорога—[дарогъ]—road
Поворот—[пъварот]—turn
Волочить—[въЛачит']—to drag
Облако—[облъкъ]—cloud

Pretonic **A** is sometimes represented in phonetic notation as [**Λ**]**,** but the standard [**A**] is adequate here. The main purpose of our treatment of colloquial phonetics here is to illustrate the phonetic processes involved in colloquial speech, to show they are systematic, and to give examples of some forms of words or expressions a student might hear.

Scholarly interest in colloquial pronunciation has gone through several stages, increasing in specificity as the years progressed. L.V. Shcherba is credited with introducing into Russian phonetics the concept of pronunciation styles.[65] For the sake of simplicity, he chose to delineate two styles: *полный* (full) and *разговорный* (colloquial). His bipartite division received wide acceptance in Russian linguistic literature and was the basis for the treatment of pronunciation styles in the 1952-54 *Academy Grammar*. There, full-style pronunciation is described as varying from that of a lecturer in a large auditorium, or a radio announcer, to that of a speaker in everyday speech who wishes to emphasize a word:

- **Ну и что же вы на это ему ответили?**
- **Ни-че-го!** (ГрамРЯ:55)

So how did you answer him to that?
No-thing!

Colloquial pronunciation, however, reveals a series of gradations in the direction away from the very articulate and towards sub-standard. Therefore, researchers of CR pronunciation often speak in relative terms, that is, an item may be 'more colloquial' or 'less colloquial.' According to Shcherba, "...corresponding to the variety of social conditions for speech, one can distinguish a multitude of styles."[66] *The Academy Grammar* supported this conclusion in recognizing various degrees of 'colloquialness' in pronunciation. It stated: "the colloquial style presents an even wider selection of versions and, therefore, is more of a relative matter."[67] An example used by the *Grammar* is the greeting ***Здравствуйте, Александр Александрович!*** In the average colloquial pronunciation, this greeting would be pronounced:

[*здраст'ь ал'ьсан ал'ьсанч*]

The extreme variant of colloquial pronunciation would be:

[***здрась сан санч***] (ГрамРЯ:56)

The first edition of R.I. Avanesov's *Русское литературное произношение* (1954) represented the next step toward defining pronunciation styles with greater specificity.[68] He devoted several pages to the subject. Although, like his predecessors, Avanesov found it necessary to simplify somewhat his presentation, he did include one additional category. From a wide range of such styles as "poetic," "oratorical," "academic" (or "bookish"), "colloquial" and "substandard," he chose the following tripartite scheme:

bookish - книжный
colloquial – разговорный (стилистически нейтральный)
substandard – просторечный

Avanesov's presentation might lead one to think he was shying away from real colloquial speech. He used the terms "neutral" and "colloquial" to define the same style, which is a bit incongruous, since 'neutral' is usually understood to mean 'colorless,' 'unemotional,' 'non-expressive' speech. Avanesov apparently sensed the need for further clarification, since he subsequently divided colloquial style into "strict" (*строгий*) and "free" (*свободный*). Strict refers to the pronunciation of the stage where, although the speech is based on colloquial style, the theater "maintains stricter allegiance to [KLJ] pronunciation norms; maintains more firmly the established and historically outdated norms. It does not accept many of the new developments in pronunciation which are formed in everyday, direct speech."[69]

In 1963, a rather detailed treatment of pronunciation styles was published in an article by M.V. Panov—«*Русское литературное произношение*».[70] This article was to serve as the forerunner to a volume dedicated to phonetics in РЯСО. Panov provides many examples and enumerates with considerable detail the phonetic changes that may occur in colloquial pronunciation. His stylistic scheme is tripartite:

высокий	high
нейтральный	neutral
разговорный	colloquial

Under the influence of these studies by Panov, Avanesov revised his *Русское литературное произношение* to reflect Panov's stylistic scheme, writing in the preface of his later volume:

> I took into account the works of my student M.V. Panov, in particular, his article "On Styles of Pronunciation"... His conclusions on the delineation of pronunciation styles turned out to be so significant, that it was impossible to ignore them in preparing this edition.[71]

It's important to reiterate that there are many phonetic gradations in CR, depending on the speaker and the situation. G.A. Barinova provides a detailed example of the various possible gradations of the word *Здравствуйте*. Here is an abbreviated version of how she illustrates this:

[здравствуйт'и^{э}]
[здрас'т'ь]
[здрас'т']
[зрас'т']
[драс'т']

[рас'т']
[зъс']
[зс']
[с']
(Бар 1973:122*)*[72]

DELETION

The most important characteristic of colloquial pronunciation is the tendency to reduce the contrast among segmentals. This reduction may be complete, that is, a sound may disappear (what we call here 'deletion'). This reduction/deletion may take many forms. Vowels and consonants behave differently. Despite a wide range of gradations, certain patterns can be identified.

The gradations are important because the same word may be pronounced several ways. The examples below have been recorded on tape or by hand by Russian linguists. They are given as proof of the systematic character of deletion in CR. Another factor to consider when listening to colloquial speech is the position of a word in the stream of the utterance. The farther away a word is from utterance stress, the more likely there will be significant deletions among the segmentals.

Vowels

Russian vowels maintain their full value only under stress, although the vowels [**У**], [**И**], [**Ы**] [**Э**] may, when not stressed, be reduced so slightly that it is negligible for the student. The orthographic vowels **О, А, Е, and Я** are, when not stressed, significantly changed or are deleted—even is KLJ. In CR, however, the change is often much more widespread and severe. Some deletion patterns are illustrated in the examples below.

First pre-tonic position. The vowel in the first pre-tonic position may be deleted. This occurs most often when the vowel follows a palatalized consonant and is not itself the first vowel in the word:

	[ун'ив'ърс'тет]	университет	university
or	**[ун'ирс'тет]**		
	[вун'ирс'тет'ь]	в университете	at the university

[пр'исъ'ид'няус']	присоединяюсь	I join
[к'итъ], [к'ит]	какие-то	some kinds of
[сстра]	сестра	sister

(Бар 1973:45)

First post-tonic position. Reduction to zero (deletion) is most widespread in the first post-tonic position:

[комнтъ]	комната	room
[холдна]	холодно	cold
[пожалста]	пожалуйста	please
[двацц]	двадцать	twenty

(Бар 1973:46)

Second post-tonic position. Generally speaking, the second post-tonic vowel is least likely to be deleted. There are two situations where this does, however, occur: (1) in very frequent words, such as patronymics, and (2) when the second pre-tonic syllable begins with the sonorants **Л, Р**:

[якл'нъ]	Яковлевна	patronymic
[д'м'итр'ьч]	Дмитриевич	patronymic
[провълкъ]	проволока	wire
[папърт'н'ик]	папоротник	fern

(Бар 1973:47)

Other positions. Barinova notes that words having more than three pre- or post-tonic syllables were quite rare in the informants' material. Some examples, however, are provided here of words frequently used in the classroom:

[к$^{(ъ)}$ръндаша]	карандаша	pencil (gen. case)
[б'л'иатекъ]	библиотека	library

(Бар 1973:48)

The role of palatalized consonants in the deletion of vowels is significant. Many examples of vowel deletion are noted when the vowel follows or is between palatalized consonants. Note some consonants also are deleted:

[выход’ти^{э}]	выходите	you go out
[вид’ма]	видимо	apparently
[д’ис’(т’в)ит’на]	действительно	actually
[преж’ш’ьм]	прежде чем	before
[ч’ра]	вчера	yesterday
[д’и^{э}с’ти]	десяти	ten (gen. case)

(Бар 1973:50)

After sonorants and in conjunction with fricatives, similar deletion may occur.

Perhaps one of the most remarkable features presented by Barinova about colloquial phonetics is the qualitative changes that may occur in vowels *under stress*. This occurs most often after palatalized consonants. Even native speakers can misunderstand an utterance due to what these vowels sound like. For example, there may be some confusion between **А** and **Э**, as demonstrated by the following errors in hearing:

Spoken — **Сеточку взять надо.**
[We] have to take the net
Heard — **Десяточку?**
(Бар 1973:62)
A tenth?

Also possible confusion between **Е** and **И**:

Spoken — **Завтра к десяти я должна идти в милицию.**
By ten tomorrow I have to go to the police.
Heard –– **На какую лекцию?**
(Бар 1973:63)
To what lecture?

Stressed **О** may sound like **У**:

Spoken — **в то лето**
In that summer

Heard — **в туалет**
(Бар 1973:64)
To the toilet

Consonants

Although consonants are more stable than vowels in CR, they also are subject in some cases to deletion. Such deletion does occur in KLJ, usually as a simplification of consonant clusters, but it occurs more often in CR. Especially when the consonants are intervocalic.

Intervocalic Consonants

In CR, the intervocalic palatalized consonant **Д** is frequently deleted:

Он каждый день здесь [прахоит]	**проходит**
Юра сейчас [выит]	**выйдет**
Она давно там [нахоиццъ]	**находится**

(Зем 1987:195)

The same phenomenon may occur after other consonants in different parts of speech:

[съ^{и}ршэна]	совершенно
[с'иодня]	сегодня
[праъ^{э}л'нъ]	правильно
[каэшъ]	конечно
[каъцъ]	кажется
[вашше]	вообще
[с'иа]	себя

(Зем 1987:195)

Consonant Cluster Simplification

In CR many consonant clusters are simplified:

[фстр] > [стр]	**[$^{\text{(ф)}}$стретит']**	встретить / to meet
[фст] > [ст]	**[$^{\text{(ф)}}$стат']**	встать / to stand/get up
[кст] > [кс]	**[ксати]**	кстати / by the way
[тлн] > [тн]	**[выраз'ит'на]**	выразительно / expressively

[лдн] > [лн] **[холна]** холодно / cold
[рш] > [ш] **[съшэнъ]** совершенно / completely
(Бар 1973:88-90)

In general, voiceless consonants are deleted easier than voiced, non-palatalized easier than palatalized, stops easier than fricatives, and most of all—voiceless fricatives.

Deletion of Г, Л

It's very common for a **Г** or **Л** to be dropped in high frequency words:

[када] когда / when
[тада] тогда / then
[токъ] только / only
[стокъ] столько / so many
[скокъ] сколько / how many
[несъкъ] несколько / several
(Бар 1973:91)

Deletion of **Ф** or **В** may occur in several consonant combinations:

[са^{ф}сем] совсем / completely
[п'ърид'и] впереди / ahead / in the front
[насяк'ь] на всякий (случай) / in any (case)
[прадъ] правда / truth
[дано] давно / ago
[перъвъ] первого / first (gen. case)
(Бар 1973: 93)

Consonants and Vowels in Phrases.

As noted above, the deletion of consonants and vowels is sometimes determined by factors that go beyond the word unit. Most important is the phrase stress. A vowel, which may be stressed in an individual word may not be stressed in a phrase. The following are some common phrases and expressions with their phonetic representation in CR:

[зъч'так]	значит, так / that means so
[нъч']	значит / that means
[таксът']	так сказать / so to say
[онгът]	он говорит / he says
[покраймнетъ]	по крайней мере мне-то / at least as far as I'm concerned
[с'орэм'ъ]	все время / all the time
[сърано]	все равно / it doesn't make any difference
(Бар 1973:44, 93)	

ADDITION: VOWEL INSERTION BETWEEN CONSONANTS

There are also rare instances of addition, that is, the insertion of vowels between certain consonants. This makes the word easier to pronounce. (Beginning students incorrectly do this with some words such as *много*, saying [*мъногъ]):

[фил'ьм]	фильм / film
[рубъл']	рубль / ruble
[т'атър]	театр / theater
(Бар 1973:91)	

The above examples illustrate the problems a student of Russian may encounter in attempting to understand live, spoken CR. These examples may be extreme variants, compared to what they would be in KLJ. Educated native speakers of Russian often use forms that are not always so extreme, but the forms in the above examples *are* used and are acceptable.[73]

One might be inclined to attribute the appearance of the phonetic reductions shown above solely to the rate of speech. It is only natural that colloquial speech is usually conducted at a faster rate than that of an official government announcement or a public lecture. Although speech rate does have some influence on pronunciation, it is not always the determining factor. Panov points out that "an individual, wishing to speedily relay official instructions to subordinates, could do so at a high rate of speech, but without the phonetic peculiarities of colloquial speech." (Пан 1963:23)

PHONETICS OF INTRODUCTORY WORDS AND PHRASES

Taking into account both vowels and consonants, the following are examples from a list Zemskaya provides of the most commonly used words and phrases with their possible colloquial pronunciation (some of which are also shown above):[74]

Вдруг	**[друк]**		
Вообще	**[вапшше]**	**>[вашше**	**>[шше]**
В самом деле	**[фсамдели]**		
Все-таки	**[сётки]**		
Давно	**[дано]**		
Здравствуйте	**[здрасс'ти]**		
Значит	**[знач]**	**>[начит]>**	**>[нач]**
Как сказать	**[кскът']**		
Когда	**[када]**	**>[каа]**	
Между прочим	**[межу прочим]**		
Может быть	**[можбыт']**	**>[мобът']**	
Несколько	**[несъкъ]**	**>[неска]**	
Очень	**[очн']**	**>[ош'н']**	
Потому что	**[птуштъ]**		
Сегодня	**[сёдня]**	**>[сёня]**	
Сейчас	**[сичас]**	**>[шш'ас]**	
Спасибо	**[пасибъ]**		
Так сказать	**[тскът']**		
Только	**[тока]**		
Честное слова	**[чеслова**		

<u>Numbers</u>

Двадцать	**[двацц]**
Десять	**[дест']**

Пятьдесят	**[пиисят]**	**>[п^{ь}сят]**
Семьдесят	**[сем'сит]**	
Тысяча	**[тышша]**	
Шесть	**[шес']**	
Шестьдесят	**[ш^{ъ}сят]**	

Pronouns

Каждый	**[кажый]**	
Кто-нибудь	**[ктонит']**	
Меня	**[мя]**	
Себя	**[ся]**	
Тебе	**[те]**	
Тебя	**[тя]**	
Что-то/чего-то	**[чёта]**	

Verbs

Выйдет	**[выдит]**	**>[выит]**
Говорю	**[гру]**	
Говорит	**[грит]**	
Ездить	**[езит']**	
Поедешь	**[паеиш]**	
Смотрю	**[смарю]**	

(Зем 1987:206-207)

INTONATION

The fact that segmentals can be so severely reduced and communication still continues is due to two major factors. First, the linguistic and situational contexts limit the possibilities for interpretation of an utterance. Secondly, intonation carries a considerable portion of the information. Intonation may play an important role, for example, in interpreting the question ***Который час***? According to Vinogradov, this question may mean "Why are you so late?" or "Why don't you leave?" or "My God, how boring!" "It seems I'm late," etc.[75]

Intonation, then, is crucial in CR. It's an important determinant of the syntax and word order of CR utterances. C. Boyanus and N. Jopson were perhaps the first to identify the four primary types of intonation in 1952.[76] John R. Baldwin introduced the concepts of pause and hesitation in his 1979 study of intonation. The most well-known synchronic study of intonation by Soviet/Russian scholars, however, came to light in 1963 by E.A. Bryzgunova. Her work continues to this day to be a basis for the study of the subject by many scholars. Although her work dealt primarily with standard, neutral speech, many of her findings still form the starting point in the study of colloquial intonation.[77]

T. Shustikova believes that for intonation to be classified as colloquial, it must be accompanied by colloquial vocabulary and grammar.[78] Barinova goes a little farther in attributing specific characteristics to colloquial intonation.[79] She agrees with Shustikova that the basic patterns are the same in both KLJ and CR, but maintains that in CR:

(1) there are more variants of the patterns;

(2) the contrasts between highs and lows (amplitude of modulation) are more pronounced; and

(3) the patterns alternate more often and, thus, CR demonstrates much less monotone than KLJ.

Perhaps the earliest significant study of intonation specific to CR appeared in RRR-70, where there are four articles devoted to it.[80]

SUMMARY OF COLLOQUIAL PHONETICS

To observe and analyze sound in the speech stream presents, even under the best experimental conditions, many difficulties. For example, Panov reports, "the fact that *есть* and *десять* can be pronounced identically in colloquial style proved to be an unexpected and surprising discovery."[81] Another problem is the fact that the slightest external factor (e.g. a microphone, suspicion or knowledge that one is speaking to a linguist, etc.) often triggers a shift in pronunciation, be it ever so slight. Still more difficult is it to discuss phonetics (including intonation) based on secondary sources, regardless of how reliable they are.

Nevertheless, one can attain a general overview of the patterns of phonetics in CR. The primary factor is reduction/deletion. The foreign student should take this into account upon contact with live Russian speech. Confronted with colloquial intonation, the student should have less difficulty, if he or she knows the situation and has mastered the basic intonation patterns of KLJ (the *ИК*s of Bryzgunova).

CHAPTER 5

Morphology

Morphology deals with the description and study of word forms. Since this includes inflection, the Russian language has a complex network of morphological forms. The study of colloquial morphology is, however, somewhat difficult because, according to Zemskaya, "Unlike syntax, phonetics and word formation, colloquial morphology displays fewer contrasts with KLJ."[82] Partly as a result of this, the serious study of colloquial morphology was not undertaken for several years. Most early scholars treated colloquial morphology in Russian as being simply a matter of inflectional variation in the masculine-genitive case and in the formation of plural for certain masculine nouns.

But there is more to colloquial morphology than the two elements described above.

E.V. Krasilnikova argues that not only does CR use forms and usages uncharacteristic of KLJ, but the result is that CR presents a *systemic* change from that in KLJ. According to her, the reduction of a number of certain morphologic forms, e.g., participles (*причастия*), gerunds/verbal adverbs (*деепричастия*) and short adjectives, results in certain changes in the overall morphologic system. Not only does the use of CR presuppose certain selection criteria of forms, words and structures, but the internal, paradigmatic relationship of these forms, words and structures is qualitatively different. For example, if in CR the long participle and gerund/verbal adverb are used rarely, then the main verbal contrast remaining is infinitive vs. personal forms. This makes the verb paradigm analogous to the nomen paradigm, in that now the relationship is simply infinitive vs. inflected forms of the verb, just as the nomen paradigm is nominative vs. inflected forms.[83]

Below are some morphologic characteristics of parts of speech in CR.

NOUN

Genitive Case Endings for Some Masculine Singular Nouns

D. E. Rozental devotes four pages to the variation in masculine-genitive case (sometimes referred to as the 'partitive genitive') **У** instead of **А** and five to the formation of masculine plural **А** instead of **Ы**.[84] Panov, in the РЯСО volume *Морфология Синтаксис* devotes a chapter to the same items. After examining selected printed works in KLJ in a longitudinal study of 19th and 20th century usage, and conducting extensive contemporary questionnaires by age group, Panov reported in РЯСО that since the turn of the 20th century, the use of thc ending **У** in KLJ has decreased.[85]

Rozental points out that the **А** suffix predominates today in the speech of young people. The suffix **У** may, therefore, be viewed as 'more colloquial' since it deviates from the tendency in KLJ to use **А**. It's possible then that eventually **У** will be used primarily in fixed expressions of the type **с глазу на глаз** (eye to eye), **сбиться с толку** (confuse, muddle), **что есть духу** (at full speed) or as a partitive genitive formed from diminutives **выпить чайку, коньячку** (have a drink of tea, cognac). In the above common expressions, themselves used most frequently in CR, and in the diminutives (used almost exclusively in CR) the **У** is mandatory.[86]

Plural of Some Masculine Nouns in CR

Nominative plural of some masculine nouns is the other inflectional suffix referred to above. Historically, the use of **А** was apparently quite rare in KLJ. Lomonosov noted only three words with **А** as the standard plural suffix:

бок—бока / side(s)
глаз—глаза / eye(s)
рог—рога / horn(s)
(Роз 1968:112)

He noted a few words that could use either suffix, among which were:

берег—береги—берега / bank(s), shore(s)
колокол—колоколы—колокола / bell(s)

лес—лесы—леса / forest(s)
луг—луги—луга / meadow(s)
остров—островы—острова / island(s)
снег—снеги—снега / snow(s)
(Роз 1968:112)

Over the years, this number has increased steadily so that now there are about two hundred words that may take either ending.[87]

Where there is a choice between the two forms, the use of **А/Я** usually carries a more colloquial flavor. This is illustrated by the following two examples, where **А/Я** is used in dialogue and **Ы/И** in the author's narrative:

Вот здесь, за нефтбаками, наши сейнера, сказал Вольнов… Они пошли вниз, к реке, от которой пахло мазутом, там отшвартовывались возле гнилых свай сейнеры.
(Пан, РЯСО Морф 1968:204.)

"Now here, behind the fuel tanks, are our seiners," said Volnov… They went down to the river, which stank of oil. There the seiners were moored next to the rotten piles.

-Слезари прикрепили к полу станки и моторы…
-Верно, три года мы с тобой проучились и вышли слесаря-ремонтировщики третьего разряда.
(Пан, РЯСО Морф 1968: 203-204)

-The metal workers were fastening the mounts and motors to the floor.
-That's right, for three years you and I trained and then became metal repairmen third-class."

Panov suggests two other factors, which indicate the colloquial nature of several plurals in **А/Я**. Due in part to editors' demands, the **Ы/И** form predominates in standard, written, official publications (technical manuals, reference books, etc.). On the other hand, in modern poetry, which traditionally uses many elements of CR and is less subject to editors, the use of **А/Я** is widespread.[88]

The other factor pointing to the 'colloquialness' of **А/Я** derives from the findings of questionnaires given to various social and age groupings on this very subject. When asked to complete some sentences of the type **К причалу**

подходили военные катер___ (The military cutters approached the mooring), the resultant responses varied considerably. Briefly stated, manual laborers, white-collar workers and non-language students were more likely to use **А** than **Ы**. At the other end of the spectrum were linguists, writers and journalists, who were more likely to use **Ы**. Likewise, when called upon to make a conscious evaluation of these two possible suffixes, as in "Which of the given phrases seems the more correct to you? — **В порту стояли крейсеры, В порту стояли крейсера** (Cruisers stood in the port)"—many groups preferred the form **А**. The one exception was the group of writers and journalists, whose preference was toward **Ы**. It's interesting to note that many writers and journalists who indicated a preference for **Ы** often used **А** in their own speech.[89]

Vocative Case

One of the most interesting features of colloquial morphology is that it presents an additional noun case to the six that already exist in KLJ: the vocative case. This case is used as a form of address. Many modern Indo-European languages (English, Spanish, etc.) have lost the vocative case, but others retain it, including the Baltic languages, some Celtic languages and several Slavic languages, including Ukrainian.[90] Russian lost the historic vocative except for such words as *Отче, Боже!, Господи!*, which, as can be seen, are of religious (OCS) origin.

A new vocative, however, has developed in Russian.[91] Names that end in **А** or **Я** are made into vocative case by dropping the last vowel. This is used with proper names and some family terms:

Мама	**Мам!**
Папа	**Пап!**
Юра	**Юр!**
Петя	**Петь!**
Вася	**Вась!**
Дядя Коля	**Дядь Коль!**
Тётя Соня	**Тёть Сонь!**
(Зем 1987:77-79)	

Саш / ты можешь вместо пиджака надеть кофту серую?
(Лап 1976:211)

Sash, instead of the jacket could you put on the grey cardigan?

Пап / а у тебя здесь гвоздики маленькие есть?
(Лап 1976:210)
Pop, you have any small nails here?

Па / где же вот здесь вот кусок отвалился?
(Лап 1976:266)
Pa, where did this piece go that fell off?

Ма / кто там написал лошадь у нас в маленьком домике висит?
(Лап 1976:298)
Ma, who drew the horse that hangs in the small house?

Other classes of words do not have a vocative. There are, however, some plural vocative forms, such as *ребят, девушк*—forms of address for *ребята* and *девушки* (guys, gals).

Ребята / а ребят / вон там байдарки идут еще //
(Лап 1976:147)
Boys, hey guys. There's another canoe over there.

Девушк / а где еще можно посмотреть вазы?
(Лап 1976:149)
Girls, where else can one see vases?

VERB

Several scholars maintain that the gerund/verbal adverb (*деепричастие*) is very seldom used, except for such frequent references to a person's status/condition: *сидя, лежа, стоя*. But many gerund forms are still found in CR, especially in negation, as seen from these phrases:

Не вдаваясь в подробности
(Зем 1973:169)
Not going into detail

Не сходя с этого места
(Зем 1973:169)
Not leaving this place

Идти не оглядываясь
(Зем 1973:170)
Walking without looking around

Говорить не переставая
(Зем 1973:170)
Talking incessantly

Говорить не думая
(Зем 1973:170)
Speaking without thinking

Не зная в чем дело / она берется судить //
(Зем 1973:168)
Not knowing what's going on, she starts judging.

Я прожил там шесть месяцев / ничего не делая //
(Зем 1973:168)
I lived there six months doing nothing.

Both expressions *не смотря на...* (despite) and *смотря на...* (it depends on) are frequent:

Не смотря на воспитание/все равно очень хороший ребенок //
(Зем 1973: 172)
Despite his upbringing, he's really a good child.

Пойдете в кино?
Смотря на что //
(Зем 1973: 172)
Are you going to the movie?
It depends.

In CR a verb form that looks like an imperative may be used when expressing sudden, momentary action. (In Russian, called *прошедшее мгновенно-произвольное действие.*) It is singular and is often accompanied by heightened intonation:

Дорога ровная / а он возьми и упади //
(Зем 1987:87)
The road is level, but he up and fell.

Also referring to what one might have been:

Приди я вовремя / ничего бы не случилось //
(Зем 1987:88)
Had I come in time, nothing would have happened.

Не проспи он / не опоздал бы на поезд //
(Зем 1987:88)
If he hadn't overslept, he wouldn't have been late to the train.

One finds also in CR an expressive imperative form meaning just the opposite of its semantic meaning. (Zemskaya provides the meaning.)

Поговори мне только! (Замолчи)
(Зем 1987:90)
Be quiet!

Опоздай хоть на пять минут! (Не опаздывай)
(Зем 1987:90)
Don't be late by even five minutes!

When the imperative is used in its normal meaning in CR, it's usually accompanied by a pronoun:

Ты возьми себе мясо в холодильнике //
(Зем 1987:89)
Get yourself the meat in the refrigerator.

One misconception about verbal usage in CR is that it uses special verbs to indicate repetitive actions in the distant past, such as *хаживал, читывал*. This is not the case. In modern CR one finds instead:

ходил давно и не один раз
(Зем 1987:88)
A long time ago he went often.

читал когда-то много раз
(Зем 1987:88)
In the past he read many times.

Zemskaya describes such verbs as *хаживать* and *читывать* when they are used in literary works, as an attempt at "imitation of colloquial speech."

The use in CR of verbs ending in–ничать or -ствовать formed from nouns may reflect also a sarcastic or negative connotation:

Интеллигентничаете, лейтенант.
(Пан, РЯСО Словообр 1968:235)
You are acting like an intellectual, Lieutenant.

Что они делают – бандитничают.
(Пан, РЯСО Словообр 1968:235)
What they're doing is acting like bandits.

Сейчас развелось немалое количество вознесенствующих, евтушенствующих и ахмадулинствующих молодых поэтов.
(Пан, РЯСО Словообр 1968:235)
Now there has developed no small number of Voznesenky-like, Evtushenko-like and Akhmadulina-like young poets.

Panov suggests that if verbs in both *–ничать* and *–ствовать* are useable, the former would be more colloquial. His conclusion is difficult to assess, however, since among his illustrative examples—*самовольничать / самовольствовать* (act willfully), both the dictionaries of Smirnitsky and Ozhegov list *самовольничать* as colloquial, but do not list the other verb at all. (Both are listed in Dal, but are not marked for style.)

Occasionally, in CR the perfective form of a verb is used when the action is actually usual and often. This can occur with both past and future tenses:

(A mother talks about her daughter's behavior.)
Она обычно как? Послушала меня и ушла // А толку никакого // (Зем 1987:89)

What does she do? She listens and goes on her way. Nothing comes of it.

Or sometimes the perfective indicates something that hasn't happened but is characteristic of the person talked about:

Маша всегда что-нибудь некстати расскажет //
(Зем 1987:89)

Masha will always start talking about something irrelevant.

ADVERB

The adverb in Russian presents a series of different morphologic forms, deriving from base words by various means. For example*, минтингово* < *минтинг, юридически* < *юридический, по-московски* < *московский, книжно, по-книжному* < *книжный*. Of primary interest for CR are those adverbs derived from base words with the aid of the suffix **–о** contrasted with the combination prefix **по-** plus suffix **-ому**. These adverbs are often derived from the same base word. Essentially the adverbs are synonymous; where earlier there may have been an adverb only in **-о (честно),** now a synonym exists (**по-честному**).

Consequently, since both forms have the same meaning, the contrast becomes much more pronounced. Adverbs in **по-…ому** are to a greater degree colloquial, while those in **–о** are correspondingly bookish or neutral. True, certain of these **по-…ому** forms have become so commonplace that they have only a slightly colloquial flavor and are often found in KLJ. For example:

по-честному	honestly
по-хорошему	well, fine
по-молодому	in a young manner
по-серьезному	seriously

по-указанному	the way it was indicated
по-особенному	especially

(Пан РЯСО Словообр 1968:248)

Others are more colloquial:

по-тупому	thick-headedly
по-хитрому	slyly
по-быстрому	fast
по-простому	simply
по-точному	precisely

(Пан РЯСО Словообр 1968:248)

Panov points to a relatively recent development in the function of adverbs in ***по-…ому***, beginning to be widespread only in the 1950s and 1960s—their pre-adjectival use to further qualify or modify the adjective. For example:

по-милому лукавые глаза
(Пан, РЯСО Словообр 1968:249)
sweetly devilish eyes

по-молодому здоровые зубы
(Пан, РЯСО Словообр 1968:250)
young-like healthy teeth

ADJECTIVE

Adjectives are used less in CR than in KLJ. For example, in a 1,000-word corpus of CR, adjectives were used only 39 times. In comparison, written scientific Russian (KLJ) used 152 and belles-letters 82 adjectives.[92] When used in CR, they often express a speaker's attitude toward an object rather than describe it. For example, the KLJ utterance **По ярко-голубому небу плывут белые облака** (White clouds are sailing through the bright blue sky) in CR would most likely be: **Ой! Какое голубое небо! А облака-то! Белые-белые!** (O! What a blue sky. And the clouds! They're so white.) (Зем 87:86)

Adjectives in CR are usually used as predicates.

A special class of possessive adjectives is formed with the suffixes **ов** and **ин** from personal names: *мамин, папин, отцов*:

А вот у маминого брата у твоего / у него жена работала?
(Лап 1976:171)
Did the wife of your mother's brother work?

Although up to the middle of the 19th century, these personal name-adjective forms occurred frequently in KLJ, today they are present for the most part only in CR and substandard speech. The exceptions are that in KLJ, one still finds some special phrases such as ***Адамово яблоко*** (Adam's apple).[93]

The most common short adjectives in CR are those that express situational, current or temporary characteristics. These are of the type *прав***,** *благодарен* and are always used as predicates:

Ну что ж / он был близок к истине //
(Зем 1973:201)
So he was close to the truth.

Ты знаком небось с ним?
(Зем 1973:201)
Any chance you know him?

Грешна // забыла // совсем из головы вылетело //
(Зем 1973:201)
My bad. I forgot. It completely slipped my mind.

Попали в милицию / и там разбирались / кто прав кто виноват //
(Зем 1973:201)
They ended up at the police station and that's where they figured out who was right and who was at fault.

Я в половине первого обязана быть дома //
(Зем 1973:201)
I have to be home at 12.30.

With some adjectives the contrast between temporary and permanent is clear:

У нас болен ребенок //
Our baby is sick.

Она больной человек была //
(Зем 1973:203)
She was a sickly person.

Some adjectives have no short form:

белый, круглый, квадратный, etc
(Зем 1973:209)

Adjectival endings and noun suffixes may even be used with abbreviations and acronyms:

ТАСС	**тассовец, тассовский**
МХАТ	**мхатовец, мхатовский**
НАТО	**натовский, натовец**

(Панов, РЯСО Словообр 1968:41)

Сел за свой упрадомский стол.
(Панов, РЯСО Словообр 1968:42)
[He] sat down at his house superintendent's desk.

Often in CR, non-KLJ adjectives are used, especially from borrowed words:

KLJ	CR
процессуальный	**процессный**
планетарный	**планетный**
комфортабельный	**комфортный**

(Панов, РЯСО Словообр 1968:59)

In fact, adjectival participles and gerunds/verbal adverbs (*причастия, деепричастия*) do occur less frequently in CR than in KLJ. The list below shows the difference in KLJ usage and that of CR:

If in KLJ it is	In CR a more likely version would be
преследующий	**который преследует**
происходящее	**что происходит**
ожидаемое	**что/чего ожидают**
(Зем 1973:415fn)	

WORD FORMATION

Russian scholars treat word formation (*словообразование*) as a separate category. This is reasonable, but it's a complex and almost inexhaustible area of CR. The sheer volume of the many possibilities of word formation makes it unlikely then that any student or textbook will find it practical to deal with it in any depth. Even Panov, whose РЯСО includes a full volume dedicated to word formation, writes "Of course, we haven't dealt with all the possible relationships of word formation and the norms of KLJ. They are complex, varied and contradictory."[94]

Russian vocabulary is replete with special words that are formed by various means for reasons of brevity or to attach special connotation to a word. Two of the most productive processes are condensed words and affixation. To some extent, both these phenomena are found in both KLJ and CR. But CR is much more productive in forming these words (and phrases). The presentation below is intended to show the major patterns of word condensation and the more frequent affixes that go into CR word formation. In many cases, word formation can be viewed as a branch of vocabulary, but since we are dealing for the most part with the colloquial variations of *words* in this chapter, we chose to include the topic here.[95]

Condensed Words

Russian has a large class of discrete two-or-more-word names that become condensed into one word. Mark T. Hooker calls this process syntactic zero (0), where a word or phrase goes to null. We call it word condensation, where the item in question is deleted. The resulting words are called in Russian *конденсаты*.[96]

Some condensed words are formed with the suffixes ***-k(a)*** and ***-lk(a)*** from the adjective in a phrase. In so doing, the noun in the phrase loses its gender and the resultant condensed word becomes feminine:

Штормовка	штормовой костюм / storm suit
Маршрутка	маршрутное такси / route taxi
Комиссионка	комиссонный магазин / commission store
Открытка	открытое письмо / postcard
Электричка	электрический поезд / electric train
(Зем 1973:409)	

According to Zemskaya, using such full phrases as *открытое письмо, электрический поезд* in normal conversation shows a lack of skill and knowledge of the language. For example, what one might expect from a foreigner. Consequently, the condensed words above are the only ones that should be used in CR.[97]

The noun suffix ***-ка*** used in condensed words may cause confusion for the student. First of all, several condensed words may be homonyms:

Комсомолка	1. a girl in the Komsomol
	2. the newspaper *Komsomolskaya pravda*
районка	1. area dispensary
(Зем 1973:409)	2. regional hospital

Condensed words may be partly regional or may vary in meaning or acceptability. For example, **научка** is used in Saratov, but is unusual in Moscow. There they use **фундаменталка** from **фундаментальная библиотека Академии *наук*** (Basic Library of the Academy of Sciences), which is not acceptable in Saratov. The Leningrad term **публичка** (public library) is acceptable neither in Moscow nor Saratov.[98]

Often the CR version of an adjective from KLJ, that is in itself a condensed form of an adjective-noun phrase, becomes a further condensed word. Here are examples of such adjective usage in KLJ and the corresponding *kondensat* in CR.

Adjective + Noun > Condensed Noun from the adjective:

KLJ	CR
моечная (машина)	**мойка** / washer
операционная (комната)	**операционка** / operating room
дежурная (служба)	**дежурка** / duty
курительная (комната)	**курилька** / smoking room

(Зем 1973:415)

Adjective > Condensed Noun

Sometimes the noun in an adjective-noun phrase disappears and the adjective becomes a noun:

KLJ	CR
Дипломная работа	**диплом** / graduation paper, dissertation
Хирургическое отделение	**хирургия** /surgical department
Вирусный грипп	**вирус** / viral flu
Химическая завивка	**химия**/chemical hair curling

(Зем 1973:418)

Она вирусом болеет?
(Зем 1973:418)
Does she have the flu?

Ой / в хирургию не ходите / не ходите / вам же в терапию //
(Зем 1973:418)
Oh, don't go into surgery, don't. You should go to therapy.

Some word condensates have become neutral in both KLJ and CR. Here are examples of official, neutral and words used only in CR:

Official KLJ	Neutral KLJ/CR	CR Only
генеральная репетиция	**генеральная**	**генералка**
сверхсрочная служба	**сверхсрочная**	**сверхсрочка**

попутная машина	**попутная**	**попутка**
Тургеневская библиотека	**Тургеневская**	**Тургеневка**
Самотечная площадь	**Самотечная**	**Самотека**

(Зем 1973:416)

Some 'kondensaty' refer to professions or purpose. They often use the suffix ***-ик***:

транзитник (транзитный пассажир)	Transit passenger
сезонник (сезонный работник)	Seasonal worker
киношник (кинодеятель)	Cinema person

Other suffixes for condensed words are also used:

леговушка (легковая машина)	Passenger car
черняшка (черный хлеб)	Black bread
спецуха (спецзанятие)	Special activity
штормяга (штормовой костюм)	Storm suit
деревяшка (деревянный протез)	Wooden prothesis
губнушка (губная помада)	Lipstick

(Зем 1973:416)

Affixes

In CR suffixes and prefixes are a frequent way to form new words or add various shades of meaning to a word.

Suffixes

From the above discussion of condensed words, it should be clear how important suffixes are in CR. Besides their use in condensed words, the major suffixes are usually covered in basic Russian courses, especially the expressive diminutive, augmentative and pejorative. These new, expressive nouns are formed by means of a suffix added to a neutral noun. The following examples show some of the most common expressive suffixes found in CR:

Diminutive

Suffix	Neutral Noun	New Noun	Little, Dear
-ец	брат	**братец**	brother
-ок	друг	**дружок**	friend
-чик	диван	**диванчик**	couch
-ик	гвоздь	**гвоздик**	nail
-ица	сестра	**сестрица**	sister
-ка	дочь	**дочка**	daughter
-очка	звезда	**звёздочка**	star
-ушка	голова	**головушка**	head
-енька	дорога	**дороженька**	road

Augmentative

-ище / ища	волк	**волчище**	big wolf
вино	**винище**		a lot of wine
борода	**бородища**		big beard
-ина	мост	**мостина**	big bridge

Perjorative

-онка	бумага	**бумажонка**	awful paper
-ишка	погода	**погодишка**	bad weather

(ГрамРЯ:55)[99]

A few words with pejorative suffixes may no longer have negative connotations, but rather are more endearing: *сестрёнка*—dear sister, *братишка*—dear brother.

Other Suffixes

In CR the suffixes ***-щик/-чик, -чиц, -тель*** may form nouns from verbs that refer to people who perform the verb action. (Zemskaya provides the explanations.)

Эти переснимальщики по воскресеньям не работают //
(о тех, кто делает фотокопии)
(Зем 1987:116)
The people who make copies don't work on Sundays.

Она прекрасный искатель //
(умеет искать потерянное)
(Зем 1987:116)
She's a good finder.

The suffix ***-ник*** may be added to a noun in order to describe a characteristic of the noun:

Он у нас осенник //
(родился осенью)
(Зем 1987:117)
He was born in the fall.

The suffixes ***-овец, -ник, -щик*** may also be used to designate the location of a person:

Физфаковцы (from the Physical Department)
Эмгеушник (from MGU, Moscow University)
(Зем 1987:117)

According to Patrolova, Sandzhi-Gulyaeva and Kurilova:

- The most productive suffix is **-k**. Almost 1/3 of all suffixes use **-k**;
- Affixes can be formed from verbs, adjectives and nouns;
- Condensed words are very common in CR (***научка, читалка***);
- Many words with the suffix ***-ka*** have become neutral KLJ words (***палатка, елка, привычка, девушка);***

- The suffixes **-ение -ание**, are bookish and are primarily from verbs; and
- **-ель** is used only occasionally (***помогатель, нервотрепатель***).[100]

Prefixes

As with many suffixes, prefixes should be learned like vocabulary items. They can be attached to almost any part of speech. Sometimes they are used together with suffixes. The following are some of the more frequent prefixes:

СО- together
Я встречалась со своей состуденткой //
(Зем/Китай/Шир 1981:107)
I met with my fellow student.

ПЕРЕ- repeated action
Надо ей переэкзамен устроить //
(Зем/Китай/Шир 1981:107)
We have to retest her.

ПОД- part of something
Думаешь у нее есть свои подцели?
(Зем/Китай/Шир 1981:107)
Do you think she has ulterior motives?

СВЕРХ-/ СУПЕР-/ УЛЬТРА-/ АРХИ-– high degree of something
Это сверхнаивность //
(Зем/Китай/Шир 1981:107)
That's naivete to the highest degree.

Он архидурак //
(Зем/Китай/Шир 1981:107)
He's a real fool.

ПРЕ-/ РАЗ- / НАИ- high degree
Настроение у меня преотличное //
(Зем/Китай/Шир 1981:108)
My mood is great.

БЕЗ-
This prefix is quite frequent in CR, as it is often attached to a noun to express absence:

Меня огорчает безбалконье //
(Зем 1981:75)
It bothers me not to have a balcony.

Он не переносит безгазетья //
Зем 1981:75)
He can't stand not having a newspaper.

На этой улице полное безмагазинье //
(Зем 1981:75)
There are no stores on this street.

In CR prefixes might even function as separate words if the first speaker in a dialogue uses a prefixed word:

- **Ты переспал?**
  Did you oversleep?
- **Скорее нéдо чем пере** //
  (Зем 1981:75)
  More like not enough than over.

- **Вас обсудили?**
  Did they discuss you (your work)?
- **Не об / а о** //
  (Зем 1981:75)
  Not discussed, rather critisized.

James R. Holbrook

SUMMARY OF COLLOQUIAL MORPHOLOGY

Affixes and condensation of phases are the most frequent way to form new words in CR. Other than that, taken from the point of view of the student, morphologic reflections in CR should pose little difficulty. The student should probably approach suffixes and prefixes as vocabulary items. The best description of the overall patterns in CR morphology is provided by Zemskaya in her 1987 *Русская разговорная речь: лингвистический анализ и проблемы.* Charles Townsend's *Russian Word Formation* is also helpful if the student wishes to dig deeper into this phenomenon.

CHAPTER 6

Syntax

The syntax of CR presents a very productive area of investigation, due in part to its frequent and significant deviations from the syntax of KLJ. It's not surprising, therefore, that most of the early research done on CR dealt with syntax.[101]

The syntactic system of KLJ has been very well described and its norms fixed in writing (hence, the term 'codified'). The study of colloquial syntax has most often focused on deviations from KLJ norms. Most investigators of CR have, however, noted that the more these deviations are studied, the more they appear regular and systematic. This is the theoretical framework presented by Zemskaya and others in RRR-73. Not only do they view the structure of CR as independent of KLJ, but in many instances it's so different as to necessitate a reevaluation of the traditional idea of what a syntactic structure is. In contrast to the phonetic and morphologic levels of speech, syntax is a deeply integrated conglomerate of various degrees of logic and psychology, as well as situational and linguistic context.

It is only by taking such factors into consideration, and knowing that *Бойню* refers to the novel *Slaughter House Five*, can one analyze or decode such utterances as this:

Третий «Нового мира» «Бойню» мне хочется есть у вас?
(Зем 1973:332)
(Zemskaya's translation: **Хочется прочитать роман К. Воннегута «Бойня номер пять», который напечатан в третьем номере журнала «Новый мир»)**

Do you have the third issue of *Novy Mir*? I'd like to read Vonnegut's novel *Slaughterhouse Five,* which is in the third issue.

What is remarkable is that the listener usually makes such an analysis quickly. This can be done only if colloquial syntactic patterns, combined with the appropriate linguistic and extra-linguistic indicators (for example, the vocabulary, pauses and intonation) are understood in the mind of the listener.

This chapter will present some of the regular CR syntactic patterns. Since the ultimate purpose of this book is to present CR in a format compatible with the teaching of Russian, constant reference will be made to KLJ. The effect, then, is of a contrastive analysis between CR and KLJ, and not a complete description of an autonomous CR system.

The criterion used for the selection of patterns and illustrative examples is that the feature being discussed could easily be related to the material a student of Russian might be expected to understand, based on his or her knowledge of KLJ.

This chapter will highlight three types of structures. The first will include those in which an element (or elements) usually found in KLJ is not explicitly expressed—*is deleted*—in CR. The second type will consist of colloquial structures in which some element *is added* to what would have been a KLJ utterance. The third type of structure represents utterances in which nominative case is *substituted* for what would be an oblique case in KLJ.[102]

In the following examples, the forward slash [/] indicates a pause, while [//] indicates the end of an utterance. If there is a question or exclamation mark at the end of an utterance, the two forward slashes are not used. According to Shiryaev, the [/] usually correlates to Bryzgunova's intonation contour—ИК-3—, while the [//] correlates to ИК-1.[103]

CONSTRUCTIONS IN WHICH AN ELEMENT IS DELETED

Below are illustrated several types of constructions, all of which contain deletion of some element. The deletion is possible because (1) the remaining utterance is so constructed that, formally or semantically, the deleted element is redundant, or (2) the intonation and context are such that the deleted item is not necessary.[104] A major factor here is the speech situation/context (*конситуация*), which presents all sorts of information shared by the speakers. Deletion is motivated primarily by:

1) the tendency in CR to economize linguistic expression to the maximum degree possible; or
2) to highlight the topic of discussion. (See chapter on word order below.)

Deletion of Adjectives

Sometimes an adjective is left out because the context provides the listener with what the noun refers to. (Zemskaya provides elaboration of the word in question.)

Я купила коньяк и <u>воду</u> / больше ничего //
(фруктовая или минеральная вода)
(Зем 1973:420)
I bought cognac and water, nothing more. (Fruit flavored or mineral water.)

У нас большие новости / мы теперь с <u>машиной</u> работаем //
(вычислительная машина)
(Зем 1973:420)
We have great news. We're now working with a machine.
(A calculating machine/computer.)

Вот осень Свету отдам в <u>сад</u> / тогда буду на курсы ходить //
(детский сад)
(Зем 1973:421)
In the fall I'll send Sveta to kindergarten. Then I'll take some courses.

Дорога ведет в <u>зону</u> // там значит военный городок стоит такой // (запретная/военная зона)
(Зем 1973:421)
The road leads to a [restricted] zone. That means a military installation is there.

Deletion of Subordinating Connectors

Subordinating connectors are used less frequently in CR than in KLJ. (Special note: Although rarely deleted, the connector *как* often means *когда.)*

Как он придет / сразу обедать будем //
(Зем 1987:90)
When (as soon as) he arrives, we'll have dinner.

Как он позвонит в дверь / беги / зови меня //
(Зем 1987:90)

When he rings the door bell, run and call me.

КОТОРЫЙ [105]

Subject

А подбери одеяло / у тебя на полу //
(Лап 1976:157) (которое)

Pick up the blanket, there by you on the floor.

Вымой вазу / на шкафу //
(Зем 1973:237) (которая находится / стоит)

Wash the vase there on the wardrobe.

Direct Object

А где эта книжка я вчера принес?
(Шир 1970:166) (которую)

Where's the book I brought yesterday?

А где шнурок / носила ты?
(Лап 1976:126) (который)

Where's the shoestring you were carrying?

Это что / картошка / ты положила да?
(Лап 1976:160) (которую)

What's that, potatoes you put [in], yes?

Л. ты помнишь фильм мы смотрели?
(Лап 1976:154) (который)

L., you remember the film we saw?

Дай мне синий шарф / у тебя был вроде //
(Зем 1971:261) (который)

Hand me a blue scarf like the one you had.

Принеси мои кеды / около бидона стоят //
(Лап 1969:32) (которые)
Bring my tennis shoes there by the can.

Preposition and который

У вас есть вешалка пальто вешать?
(Зем 1973:265) (на которой)
Do you have a coatrack where I can hang up a coat?

А где эта чашка / ты мне говорил?
(Лап 1976:292) (о которой)
Where's that cup you were telling me about?

Увидела / тут будочка-то / с Андреем все ходили //
(Лап 1976:294) (мимо которой)
I saw the booth here that everyone was going by with Andrei.

КОГДА

Utterance Initial

Я сегодня ехала / опять была авария //
(Лап 1976:306) (Когда я сегодня…)
When I was driving today, there was another accident.

Женька был дома / я позвонил //
(Зем 1973:322) (Когда я позвонил)
Zhenka was home when I called.

Ты упал / снег не попал в валенки?
(Лап 1976:309) (Когда ты…)
When you fell, snow didn't get in your boots?

Вы шли был дождь //
(Лап 1976:305) (Когда вы шли)
It was raining when you were walking.

Потом обратно шли я пять раз упал //
(Шир 1970:168) (Когда мы шли обратно)
When we were walking back, I fell five times.

Non-initial

Он спал / ты пришел?
(Лап РЯЗР 1-1968) (когда ты пришел)
Was he sleeping when you got there?

Горчицы в три я проходил нет //
(Зем 1973:337) (когда я проходил)
At three, when I went by, there wasn't any mustard.

Смотри сколько народу / а мы ехали / было меньше //
(Лап 1976:305) (когда мы ехали)
Look at all the people. When we rode by, there weren't so many.

Опять свет не погасили ушли //
(Крас 1971:29) (когда ушли)
Again you didn't turn off the lights when you left.

Потом это всё каникули начались / кончилось //
(Зем 1973:321) (когда каникули начались)
Then, when the vacation started, all this ended.

ПОТОМУ ЧТО

Я в больницу зуб болит еду //
(Зем 1973:325) (потому что зуб болит)
I'm going to the hospital because I have a toothache.

Выключи ничего интересного радио//
(Зем 1973:331) (потому что ничего интересного нет)
Turn off the radio because there's nothing interesting on.

Хлеба в магазин пойду надо мне //
(Зем 1973:326) (потому что мне надо купить хлеб)
I'm going to the store because I have to buy some bread.

Я на улице холодно не пойду //
(Шир 1970:166)　　　(потому что / если)
I'm not going out because it's cold.

ЕСЛИ

Я подольше с ним погуляю / дождя не будет //
(Зем 1981:239)　　　(если дождя не будет)
I'll walk with him longer if it doesn't rain.

Ивановы в девять / пароход не опоздает / приедут //
(Зем 1973:334)　　　(если пароход не опоздает)
The Ivanovs will be here at nine if the boat isn't late.

Я прочту / время будет / обязательно //
(Зем 1973:334)　　　(если время будет)
I'll definitely read it, if I have time.

Потеплей станет / пойдем на пляж //
(Зем 1981:236)　　　(если потеплей станет)
If it warms up, we'll go to the beach

Я попаду на Речной вокзал туда пойду?
(Лап 1976: 312)　　　(если я туда пойду)
If I go that way will I end up at River Station?

ЧТО

Жалко девчонки уезжают очень //
(Лап 1976:198)　　　(что девчонки уезжают)
It's too bad [that] the girls are leaving.

Ты забыл я тебе говорил?
(Лап 1976:321)　　　(что)
Did you forget what I told you?

Я слышала передавали по радио //
(Лап 1976: 322)　　　(что передавали)
I heard what was on the radio.

ГДЕ

Парикмахерская не скажете?
(Зем 1973:257) (где парикмахерская)
Can you tell me where the barbershop is?

А вы не знаете / Графский переулок?
(Лап 1976:160) (где Графский переулок)
You don't happen to know where Grafsky Lane is?

Вы не скажете обувная мастерская?
(Лап 1976:160) (где обувная мастерская)
Can you tell me where there's a shoe repair shop?

Deletion of Verb

Verbs are often deleted in CR. Due mainly to context and syntactic governance, they're often not necessary to the understanding of an utterance. For example, verbs are often deleted when other elements of an utterance clearly denote the object of the action as in *Я домой* // (I'm going home).

Завтра я в театр //
(Зем 1973:300) (Завтра я иду…)
Tomorrow I'm going to the theater.

Куда на каникулы?
(Сир 1968:72) (Куда вы/ты едете/едешь…)
Where are you going for vacation?

Саша / если спросят / я обедать //
(Зем 1973:301) (я пошел обедать)
Sasha, if anyone asks, I've gone to eat.

Она его на каток по средам и пятницам //
(Зем 1973:303) (Она его водит…)
She takes him to the rink on Wednesdays and Fridays.

Мою ручку / ты куда вчера?
(Зем 1973:303) (…куда положил…)
Where did you put my pen yesterday?

Она в школу по-моему с шести лет //
(Зем 1973:303) (…поступила/ходит в школу…)
She’s been going to school, I think, since she was six.

Я вот если можно / в это кресло //
(Зем 1973:303) (сяду в это кресло)
I’ll just sit in this armchair if that’s all right.

Он на вратаря-то как //
(Зем 1973:304) (…на вратаря бросился/напал)
Boy, did he go at the goalie!

Это вы про свою Олю?
(Зем 1973:304) (про свою Олю говорите)
That’s your Olya you’re talking about?

Об этом я потом //
(Зем 1973:304) (я потом поговорю / буду говорить)
I’ll talk about that later.

Не очень-то это интересно / ты покороче //
(Зем 1973:304) (ты покороче расскажи)
That’s not really very interesting. Make it a little shorter.

Нет / вот была бы у меня дочь / я бы ее только Анной //
(Зем 1973:305) (только Анной звал)
No. Now if I had a daughter, I’d call her simply Anna.

Вообще-то он Алешка / но Галя его все время Тигр //
(Зем 1973:305) (все время Тигр зовет)
In general, he’s Alyosha, but Galya always calls him Tiger.

А он тоже испанским?
(Зем 1973:305) (испанским занимается)
Does he study Spanish also?

Она каждое утро гимнастикой //
(Зем 1973:305) (гимнастикой занимается)
She does gymnastics every morning.

Ему вот в девятом классе сказали / Достоевский / и он тут же всего Достоевского//
(Зем 1973:305) (все сочинения Достоевского читал)
They told him in ninth grade Dostoevsky, and he immediately read everything Dostoevsky wrote.

Они что у вас? В карты?
(Зем 1973:306) (в карты играют)
What do they do at your place? Play cards?

Он у нас спортсмен / и в хоккей и в футбол //
(Зем 1973:306) (…играет)
He's our athlete. He plays both hockey and football.

Вот и эти пилюли мне врачи / помогли //
(Зем 1973:309) (…которые мне дали/прописали)
Now these pills the doctor gave me helped.

Я вам сегодня рубль / а остальные завтра //
(Зем 1973:309) (я вам дам…)
I'll give you a ruble today and the rest tomorrow.

Я пожалуй еще полкило //
(Зем 1973:309) (возьму/куплю)
I guess I'll take another half kilo.

Галя / а ты и моховики?
(Зем 1973:309) (моховики берешь/собираешь)
Galya, are you getting mushrooms too?

Он всякие опыты вот уже самостоятельно
(Зем 1973:309 (делает/проводит)
He already does all kinds of experiments on his own.

А сарайчик вы там сами или нанимали?
(Зем 1973:309) (…сделали/построили)
Did you build that shed yourself or did you hire it done?

The following utterances illustrate the use of some expressions that involve unstated, but easily anticipated, verbs:

А эти туфли ты щеткой одеждной?
(Зем 1973:307) (…ты чистишь)
Do you clean these shoes with a clothes brush?

Ты дверь там на замок?
(Зем 1973:307) (…запер на замок)
Did you lock the door?

Голову я шампунем обычно //
(Зем 1973:307) (…обычно мою)
I usually wash my head with shampoo.

Коля машину какой-то такой ядовитой краской //
(Зем 1973:307) (…краской покрасил)
Kolya painted his car with some sort of yucky paint.

А давайте заглавие карандашом //
(Зем 1973:307) (…заглавие напишем)
Let's write in the title with a pencil.

Infinitives

Там кругом вода / и я не мог к дому //
(Зем 1973:311) (не мог подойти)
There was water all around and I couldn't get up to the house.

Мне не хотелось об этом //
(Зем 1973:311) (об этом говорить/думать)
I didn't feel like talking/thinking about that.

Ирку я должна в школу / я должна ее из школы / потом я должна на стадион / со стадиона
(Зем 1973:311) (...должна привезти/отвезти)
I have to take Irka to school. I have to pick her up from school and take her to and from the stadium.

Надо бы нам с тобой в теннис хоть немножко //
(Зем 1973:311) (...немножко играть)
You and I have to play tennis, at least a little.

In many of the instances above, several different verbs could have been intended. For example, the utterance *Об этом я не буду* could be derived from any of the following:

Об этом я не буду
говорить
рассказывать
думать
волноваться
писать
читать

Context determines which verb is called for. The inclusion in an utterance of a phrase closely linked to a particular action, further restricts the possible choices. If, for instance, one were to include the expressions *карандашом* or *в жалобной книжке*, the missing verb would most probably be *писать*.

Present active participles and long, present passive participles are not generally used. For example, in KLJ one might say:

Дай палочку / лежащую около тебя //
Give me that stick that's by you.

In CR the most common expression of this would be:

Дай-ка вон около тебя палочка лежит //

The use of *который* for this utterance is possible in both KLJ and CR:

Дай палочку / которая лежит около тебя //
(Зем 1973:163)

CONSTRUCTIONS IN WHICH AN ELEMENT IS ADDED.

Economy in linguistic expression—the primary motivation for deletion in CR, due to the extra-linguistic context—is a characteristic of colloquial speech in almost all languages. Ironically, despite this, there is an opposite tendency: addition to colloquial speech of words and phrases, which in KLJ would be considered redundant or incorrect. The most common addition involves reduplication.

Reduplication

Reduplication means that an element is repeated within the utterance. The most common connotation of reduplication is emphasis or intensification of the meaning carried by the reduplicated element. Occasionally, the motivating factor is clarification. Once again, this occurs also in colloquial English.

Nouns and Pronouns

Ему меду надо дать / мед //
(Зем 1973:377)
He should be given honey. Honey

А я / я никому этого не говорил //
(Зем 1973:373)
Me, I didn't tell that to anyone.

А Толик ведь / Толик на Сахалине / в Хабаровске родился //
(Зем 1973:374)
Now Tolik, Tolik was born on Sakhalin, in Khabarovsk.

Дурак / дурак / а умный //
(Швед 1960:43)
He may be a fool, but he's smart.

Лида и я / мы с ней ели рыбку //
(Лап 1976:142)
Lida and I, we ate fish together.

Идите до леса до того //
(Лап 1965:15)
Go up to the forest. To that one.

The words may be in different cases, with the use of the nominative case to simply repeat the 'name' of an object (the so-called naming function—*назывная функция*).[106] Below, the motivation is apparently clarification:

Мне на Таганку // Таганка //
(Зем 1973:248)
I want to go to the Taganka theater. Taganka

A special construction, which consists of one word in the nominative and the other in the instrumental may signify positive emphasis on the characteristic named by the word as in *Молодец молодцом* (A fine boy/girl/chap).

It may also indicate that in spite of the characteristic or object named, something is awry:

План планом / а тридцать машин стоят //
(Швед 1960:56)
In spite of the plan, there're thirty vehicles not moving.

Adjectives and Adverbs

Reduplication of an adjective or adverb also signifies emphasis or intensification of the given meaning:

И мне жалко / жалко стало ее //
(Швед 1960:40)
And I was really sorry for her.

Verbs

When duplicated, verbs by their nature may signify not only emphasis, but also extended duration of repetition of the action:

А зуб все болит / болит //
(Швед 1960:34)
The tooth aches all the time.

Вот так-то и все // жил жил человек /да вдруг и умер //
(Швед 1960:35)
That's all there is to it. The guy lived for a long time and then suddenly up and died.

Вы тут? А я искал / искал / хотел проститься //
(Швед 1960:37)
You here? I've been looking all over for you. Wanted to say goodbye.

Витька прыгал / прыгал / как сумасшедший //
(Зем 1973:369)
Vitka jumped and jumped like a madman.

С ним не поеду / не поеду //
(Зем 1973:376)
I won't go with him. I just won't.

Слушал он меня / слушал //
(Швед 1960:39)
He listened and listened to me.

Interrogative words may be duplicated to show special meaning:

Где / где / а у нас всегда найдется //
(Швед 1960:71)
It may be hard to find, but we'll always come up with it.

Что / что / а уж одеться она не дура //
(Швед 1960:71)
She may do a lot of dumb things, but she knows how to dress.

Кто / кто / а он-то придет //
(Швед 1960:71)
I don't know if anyone else will come, but he'll come for sure.

Prepositions

The reduplication of prepositions, together with two closely linked words (adjectives or nouns) appears to be more motivated by the need for clarification, with the second post-prepositional word introduced as an after-thought or for clarification:

Ты можешь разбавить вон там / есть в бутылке в большой //
(Лап 1966:48)
You can dilute that over there in the bottle, in the big one.

Вообще представь себе // на таком было три рубля / на счетчике //
(Крас 1971:29)
Just imagine there were three rubles on that, the meter.

Noun and Pronoun in Same Clause

The addition of a pronoun to a clause, which already has the noun antecedent (or the reverse procedure) is common in CR. It also occurs in colloquial English.

Subject (nominative case)

А трамвай / он как идет?
(Зем 1973:243)
The streetcar, when does it go?

А он быстро идет / трамвай?
(Лап 1976:268)

It goes fast, the streetcar?

Наша Ева / она как конь //
(Иванч РЯНШ-1965:14)

Our Eve, she's like a steed.

Сейчас эта позиция Франции / она особенно объяснима //
(Лап 1976:142)

Now the position of France, that's especially explicable.

Он весь расшатался / этот мост //
(Лап 1976:269)

It got all rickety, this bridge.

И сегодня вечером он тоже пойдет по этой же самой улице / участковый уполномоченный //
Иванч РЯНШ 4-1965:16

And this evening he'll go again along the same street, the sector policeman.

Их много приходит в редакцию / писем с выражением благодарности //
(Иванч РЯНШ 4-1965:16

Many of them come to the editorial offices, letters of gratitude.

Я посмотрю что у нее в дипломе / у этой девочки //
(Зем 1973:245)

I'll take a look and see what's in her dissertation, this girl's.

Phrases may be duplicated to show repetition or emphasis:

А в трактире Вася рюмку за рюмкой / рюмку за рюмкой //
(Швед 1960:37)

In the tavern Vasya had one shot after another.

Я после / все равно я после обеда/только что сейчас от стола //
(Зем 1973:374)
Later, just the same, later after dinner I'll [do it]. I've just gotten up from the table.

И он вечером / вечером он конечно тоже работал //
(Зем 1973:372)
Even in the evening, in the evening he of course also worked.

CONSTRUCTIONS IN WHICH SUBSTITUTION OCCURS

Substitution of Nominative for KLJ Oblique Case

In CR syntax nominative case is very often substituted for words that in KLJ would use oblique cases. Intonation and juncture are more critical in these patterns than in deletion or addition. Seen in print, without taking these factors into consideration, the utterances often appear to be so deviant from KLJ norms that it may be difficult to believe that an educated native speaker would say them.

Nominative for Accusative

Я уже смотрела / «Война и мир» //
(Лап 1976:160) (Войну и мир)
I've already seen *War and Peace*.

Вы не видели / белая собака?
(Лап РЯЗР 3-1976) (белую собаку)
Have you seen a white dog?

Ты видела там баба?
(Лап 1976:157) (бабу)
Did you see that girl there?

Они уже неделя стоят //
(Лап 1976:160) (неделю)
They've been there for a week already.

Скажите / Красная площадь пройти / где мне можно?
(Лап 1976:163) (Красную площадь)
Tell me, how can I get to Red Square?

Мне подарили ручка светлая такая //
(Лап 1976:158) (ручку светлую такую)
They gave me a light-colored pen.

Л. подай вон сумка Анны Васильевны //
(Лап 1976:159) (сумку)
L. hand me that purse over there of Anna Vasilievna's.

Nominative for Genitive

Какая порода ваша собака?
(Зем 1981:63) (какой породы)
What kind of dog do you have?

Скажите / какой размер / резиновые пояса у вас есть?
(Лап 1976:159) (… какого размера)
Tell me, what size rubber belts do you have?

Творог в пачках нету у вас?
(Лап 1976:148) (Творога)
Do you have packets of cottage cheese?

Какой цвет эти тапки?
(Зем 1973:251) (какого цвета)
What colors do those slippers come in?

Три пакета молоко // Три молоко //
(Лап 1976:166) (молока)
Three packets of milk. Three milks.

Скажите / где здесь Министерство связи дом?
(Лап 1976:159) (дом Министерства связи)
Tell me, where's the Communications Ministry building?

Ведь она / шестьдесят восьмой год //
(Зем 1973:249) (68-го года)
After all, it's a 1968 edition. (She was born in 1968.)

Я / Ростовский университет //
(Зем 1973:249) (Ростовского университета)
I'm from Rostov University.

Вы / какая школа?
(Зем 1973:249) (какой школы)
What school are you from?

Он купил шкаф / карельская береза //
(Зем 1973:253) (…сделанный из карельской березы)
He bought a wardrobe made out of Karelian birch.

Скажите / у вас нет по три копейки / такие маленькие тетрадочки?
(Зем 1973:258) (таких маленьких тетрадочек)
Tell me, would you happen to have those small notebooks that cost three kopecks?

In the following examples, where nominative case is used in place of genitive, note that the word in question refers to food or drink, and that it is always followed by a unit of measurement:

Подайте пожалуйста / уксус бутылочку //
(Лап 1976:166) (бутылочку уксуса)
Please give me vinegar, a bottle.

Я достану молоко / бидон //
(Лап 1976:166) (бидон молока)
I'll get milk, a carton.

Там конфеты есть еще / коробка //
(Лап 1976:165) (коробка конфет)
There's still candy left there, a box.

Nominative for Instrumental

В прошлом году я с ним тоже ходила / больной зуб //
(Лап 1976:164) (с больным зубом)
Last year I went around with it, with a toothache.
(Note also here the presence of both pronoun and noun in the same clause.)

А вот Наташа сидит наш стол //
(Лап 1976:164) (за нашим столом)
So here's Natasha sitting at our table.

Вы говорили с товарищ Ивановой?
(Кост 1-1965:15) (…с товарищем Ивановой)
Have you spoken with Comrade Ivanova?

Nominative for Prepositional

Сядете на Площади революции / и доедете Автозаводская метро //
(Лап 1976:164) (доедете до Автозаводской станции метро)
You get on at Revolution Square and go until you reach Autofactory Subway Station.

Детский мир / идет он?
(Лап 1976:163) (идет до Детского мира, до магазина Детский мир)
[Does this] go to the Detsky Mir store?

Следующая сойдете?
(Зем 1973:256) (на следующей станции)
Are you getting off at the next station/stop?

Вот этот домик маленький / почтальонша наша живет //
(Лап 1976:159) (в этом маленьком домике)
It's in that little house that our mail carrier lives.

Какой этаж вы живете?
(Зем 1973:257) (На каком этаже)
Which floor do you live on?

Nominative for Dative

Пика удобнее чем звезда / но я привыкла звезда //
(Зем 1973:257) (привыкла звезде)
A lance is more convenient than a star, but I'm used to a star.

Все желающие / надо сдать книги обязательно и пройти в третий подъезд //
(Лап 1976:121) (всем желающим)
Everyone who wants to must definitely turn in their books and go to the third doorway.

Substitution of Pronoun for Noun

CR uses more pronouns than does KLJ. This is because the situation and context in speech often obviate the need to name the object. In many ways, this pronoun use is similar to English:

(In a store)
Мы вон те возьмем //
(Зем 1987:73)
We'll take those.

Заверите мне эти пожалуйста //
(Зем 1987:73)
Wrap these for me, please.

Ты эти наденешь?
(Зем 1987:73)
Are you going to put these on?

When the stress is on a pronoun itself (*он, она,* or *этот, тот*) it emphasizes the primary theme of the utterance:

<u>Он</u> опять не пришел //
(Зем 1987:74)
Once again, he didn't come.

<u>Она</u> этого не умеет // Бесполезно ее просить //
(Зем 1987:74)
She can't do that. No sense in asking her to.

Use of Такой and Какой

The adjective-type pronouns *такой* and *какой*, sometimes combined with other words, can be used as subjects:

Красивые платья там были / такие из натурального шелка //
(Зем 1987:74)
They have pretty dresses there. The kind out of natural silk.

Какой-то из соседней квартиры звонил //
(Зем 1987:74)
Someone from the neighboring apartment called.

А. Какой он?
Б. Всегда кричит /такой / но человек милый //
(Зем 1987:75)
A. What's he like?
B. Always yelling, that's how he is, but a nice person.

The use of *такой* often makes a statement more expressive:

Такой обед был! Пальчики оближешь!
(Зем 1987:74)
Such a dinner! Finger-lickin' good!

Такой вечер! Долго буду вспоминать //
(Зем 1987:74)
What a party! I'll remember it for a long time.

Такая девочка! Прелесть! Прехорошенькая!
(Зем 1987:74)
Such a girl! Exquisite! Extremely good looking!

SUMMARY OF COLLOQUIAL SYNTAX

The syntactic constructions of CR often deviate very significantly from their counterparts in KLJ. In some instances, KLJ elements appear to be missing, in which case the construction falls within what we have called in this book 'deletion.' Deletion is made possible by lexical, grammatical and situational constraints, which limit the range of interpretation. Intonation and the knowledge of other speakers also play a part. For example, in a conversation between two close friends, on a topic already being discussed, it is normal in any language to understand/anticipate what the other person is saying/will say. In Russian, this is known as '*с полуслова понять*.'

The second construction type illustrated above was of 'addition'—the presence in CR of an element that would not be desirable or acceptable in KLJ. Emphasis or clarification usually motivates addition. It presents little difficulty for comprehension, since, if anything, the added information is simply redundant and is similar to colloquial English.

Finally, a unique CR construction type presented in this chapter was that of 'substitution'—primarily the use of nominative case for what would be in KLJ oblique cases. This may be the hardest for students to get used to.

CHAPTER 7

Word Order

GENERAL

At first glance, word order in CR presents such a variegated picture that the non-native speaker of Russian may wonder if there is any system to it at all.

To fully appreciate how and why this word order differs from that of KLJ, a brief discussion of word order in general is in order. There are two primary functions of word order in Indo-European languages. One is to express the grammatical relationship of the component parts of an utterance; the other is to signal expressiveness or emphasis. This latter function is very prominent in CR.

Although word order and syntax in CR may appear similar, they are not the same. With colloquial syntax, words are often deleted, added, or the nominative is substituted for oblique cases. With word order, the grammar is usually clear and correct by KLJ standards. In the example here from the chapter on syntax for instance, the KLJ word order remains, but the connector *который* is deleted:

А где шнурок / носила ты?
(Лап 1976:126)

Where's the shoestring (that) you were carrying?

In Russian, word order is fairly free. This is due to 1) context, 2) intonation and 3) the use of the many inflected forms that show the syntactic relationships between words. For example, in the following sentences, presented out of context, the basic meaning remains the same, because of the grammatical connections between words that are shown by word inflexions, regardless of how the words are arranged:

Иван Машу видел в парке.
Иван в парку видед Машу.
Иван в парке Машу видел.
Машу видел Иван в парке.
Машу в парке Иван видел.
Машу Иван видел в парке.

This is not clear with such sentences as *Мать любит дочь* and *Дочь любит мать* because the inflections in the two words do not reveal whether they are subjects or objects.

In less inflected languages, such as English, free word order is not possible. In English, for example, changing the word order usually produces a different meaning or less than unacceptable sentences:

Ivan saw Masha in the park.
Masha saw Ivan in the park.
*Ivan Masha saw in the park.
*Ivan in the park saw Masha.

Intonation, of course, can change the meaning or emphasis of a sentence:

Иван видел Машу в *парке*.
Иван видел *Машу* в парке.
Иван видел Машу в парке.
Машу *видел* Иван в парке.

Emphasis in English can also be shown with intonation, but usually with additional information:

Ivan saw *Masha* in the park.
It was Masha, whom Ivan saw in the park.

Often in CR an utterance is interrupted to add new or clarifying information. Whereas in KLJ phrases and clauses are usually kept intact, in CR, due to the unrehearsed nature of an utterance, these phrases and clauses are often separated by elements of other phrases or clauses within the same utterance. Usually, the intonation is discrete enough so that the hearer immediately understands who or what is doing what. At other times, the grammatical relationships, expressed by word inflections, provide the necessary decoding information. We should keep in mind also that one of the causes of unusual word order is that in the flow of speech it's impossible to retrieve and change an utterance.

In written form a CR utterance may look weird. For example, the utterance:

Он машину приезжает часто теперь купил недавно//
(Zem 1973:31)

can be decoded as:

KLJ: Он недавно купил машину и часто приезжает теперь.
He recently bought a car and now drives here frequently.

In this case, *часто* can combine only with *приезжает*, not *купил*, for aspectual reasons; *недавно* cannot combine with *приезжает* for reasons of tense, but can easily be combined with *купил*.

Another example:

Надо / Катя приедет / одеться // or
Катя / одеться надо / приедет //
(Зем 1973:330)
KLJ: Катя приедет // Надо одеться //
Katya's coming. [We] have to get dressed.

The following example, taken from live speech, illustrates the kinds of utterances that might, at first glance, appear 'mixed up:'

А вот наша перед этим стоянка которая / разве там было близко от берега?
(Лап 1976:144)

By adjusting the word order to comply with the kind of word order the student is accustomed to, the KLJ version of this utterance may be interpreted as:

Разве перед этим наша стоянка была близка от берега?
Really, before that, was our park[ing lot] near the shore?

In general, a primary reason for unusual word order in CR is that, which the speaker deems the most important to communicate, is usually found at or near the beginning of the utterance.

REORDERING OF WORDS FROM THEIR KLJ POSITIONS

This section is devoted to illustrating some of the variations, which may occur in phrases in CR. A KLJ equivalent and English gloss are provided for each CR example. In some examples, you will see other manifestations of CR such as use of the nominative 'naming function,' etc.

Noun and Adjective

Normal word order in KLJ for nouns and adjectives is adjective + noun. In CR, however, the order often changes:

<u>Команды</u> <u>никакой</u> не было //
(Лап 1969:39) Никакой команды не было.
There was no team at all.

А где наши <u>бокальчики</u> <u>синенькие</u>?
(Лап 1965:15) А где наши синенькие бокальчики?
Where are our blue [wine] glasses?

Sometimes the adjective is distant from the noun it modifies:

<u>Оградку</u> они мне сделали <u>замечательную</u> //
(Зем 1973:388) Они сделали мне замечательную оградку.
The fence they made for me is remarkable.

Вот интересно посмотреть как тут <u>деревня</u> выглядит <u>настоящая</u>//
(Лап 1969:37) Вот интересно посмотреть, как тут настоящая деревня выглядит.
[It'll be] interesting to see here what a real village looks like.

А где <u>тетрадь</u> по арифметике <u>чистая</u> / а?
(Лап 1969:37) А где чистая тетрадь по арифметике, а?
Where's there an arithmetic notebook that's blank?

Even if the adjective + noun word order follows the normal KLJ pattern, the adjective and its noun can be distant from each other:

Маленьких у нас нет / а <u>средние</u> у нас есть <u>конверты</u> //
(Лап 1969:36) Маленьких у нас нет, а у нас есть средние конверты.
We don't have small ones, but we have medium envelopes.

<u>Жуткий</u> был <u>холод</u> у нас на работе //
(Лап 1976:224) Был жуткий холод у нас на работе.
It was terribly cold at work.

Да там <u>целое</u> почти <u>ведро</u>!
(Зем 1973:388 Да там почти целое ведро!
But there's almost a whole pail full there!

А вообще / <u>каторжная</u> ведь <u>работа-то</u> //
(Лап 1976:225) А вообще работа каторжная.
In general, the work is really back-breaking.

Если б он <u>мой</u> был <u>сынок</u> / тогда дело другое //
Лап 1965:18) Если бы он был мой сынок, тогда дело другое.
If he were my son, it would be different.

<u>Отдельного</u> нет у нас <u>издания</u> //
(Зем 1973: 391) У нас нет отдельного издания.
We don't have a separate edition.

Он ужасный имеет вид //
(Лап 1969:36) Он имеет ужасный вид.
He looks terrible.

Японскую принесла она грамматику //
(Зем 1973:390) Она принесла японскую грамматику
She brought a Japanese grammar.

Есть некоторые мне очень нравились вещи //
(Лап РЯЗР 1-1968) Есть некоторые вещи, которые мне очень нравились.
There are several things that I really liked.

When noun phrases are used as modifiers, they too can be distant from the noun modified:

Стол он купил из красного дерева себе //
(Зем 1973:390) Он купил себе стол из красного дерева.
He bought himself a table made from redwood.

Она слона вчера видела из Индии //
(Зем 1973: 390) Вчера она видела слона из Индии.
Yesterday she saw an elephant from India.

Подарили из черной кости ему шахматы //
(Зем 1973:390) Подарили ему шахматы из черной кости.
They presented him with a chess set made of black ivory.

In KLJ phrases where a noun modifies a noun, the second (modifying) noun is in the genitive case (*дом брата*–literally, House of my brother or My brother's house). In KLJ the modifying noun usually comes immediately after the noun modified. In CR, the noun and noun modifiers may be reordered or even inverted:

Я позвонил как раз тогда / когда у Сереги разгар был болезни //
(Лап 1976:189) Я позвонил как раз тогда, когда у Сереги был разгар болезни.
I called just when Serge's fever was at its height.

<u>Игоря</u> к нам собиралась приехать <u>мама</u> //
(Зем 1973:388) Мама Игоря собиралась к нам приехать.
Igor's mom planned to visit us.

<u>Игоря мать</u> скоро приезжает //
(Зем 1987:151) Мать Игоря скоро приезжает.
Igor's mother will soon arrive.

<u>Твоего брата</u> висит на вешалке <u>плащ</u> //
(Зем 1973:388) Плащ твоего брата висит на вешалке.
Your brother's raincoat is on the coatrack.

Adverb and Adjective

Since variations in CR word order usually are motivated by the desire to emphasize some part of the utterance, it is only natural that in phrases consisting of adverbs and adjectives, the deviation from KLJ is most often found in adverbs of intensification. As will be seen in the examples below, almost all adverbs connote some degree of 'very much.' In most cases the adverb is *очень*, which is often separated from the adjective it modifies:

<u>Очень</u> у нее <u>несчастный</u> вид //
(Лап 1969:39) У нее очень несчастный вид.
She looks very unhappy.

За 35 рублей / <u>очень</u> купили <u>приличную</u> коляску //
(Лап 1969:39) Купили очень приличную коляску за 35 рублей.
They/we bought a very nice baby carriage for 35 rubles.

Я считаю / что конкурс <u>очень</u> проходит на <u>высоком</u> уровне //
(Лап 1969:39) Я считаю, что конкурс проходит на очень высоком уровне.
I think the competition is progressing at a very high level.

У него необыкновенно была красивая жена //
(Лап 1969:38) У него была необыкновенно красивая жена.
He had an unusually pretty wife.

Страшно она рада была брошке //
(Лап 1976:195) Она была страшно рада брошке.
She was terribly happy with the brooch.

Она милая очень женщина //
(Лап 1969:38) Она очень милая женщина.
She's a very nice woman.

У меня низкое очень давление //
(Лап 1969:39) У меня очень низкое давление.
I have very low [blood] pressure.

Противоположный будет голый совершенно берег //
(Лап 1969:36) Противоположный берег будет совершенно голый.
The opposite bank will be completely empty.

Плащи красивые продавались у нас очень //
(Лап 1969:40) У нас продавались очень красивые плащи.
We were selling some very pretty raincoats.

И там потрясающая была совершенно фраза //
(Лап 1969:36) И там была совершенно потрясающая фраза.
And the phrase there was completely astonishing.

Ведь трудная же очень тема //
(Лап 1976:199) Ведь тема очень трудная.
It's a difficult topic after all.

Adverb and Adverb.

In phrases where one adverb modifies another, once again, the word *очень* or some word clearly associated with the meaning 'very much' is often used:

<u>Очень</u> было <u>жалко</u> / что он такой дурак //
(Лап 1976:238) Было очень жалко, что он такой дурак.
It was really too bad he was such a fool.

Это <u>очень</u> надо <u>срочно</u> //
(Лап 1976:237) Это очень срочно надо.
This has [to be done] right away.

<u>Очень</u> ты сегодня опоздала <u>здорово</u> //
(Зем 1973:388) Ты очень здорово опоздала сегодня.
You were really late today.

Лидунь / <u>хорошо</u> у тебя <u>очень</u> получается //
(Лап 1969:37) Лидунь, у тебя очень хорошо получается.
Liddy, it's turning out very well for you.

Народу было <u>много</u> <u>очень</u> //
(Лап 1976:240) Было очень много народу.
There were very many people.

CLAUSES

Up to this point, attention has been focused on the separation of phrase components. Variations in word order of clauses in CR are presented below according to the traditional syntactic categories of simple, compound and complex utterances. Here we will use underline and italics to show which of the constituents relate to each other.

Multiple Reordering in Simple Utterances

Одна ***очень*** **есть** ***элегантная*** **рубашка у Пети //**
(Зем 1973:390) Есть одна очень элегантная рубашка у Пети.
Petya has one very elegant shirt.

The above illustration may appear to be more complicated than it actually is. For example, all one must do in this example is to place the word *есть* at the beginning to get a neutral KLJ utterance. The following example, however, is not so simple:

Мы сейчас с тобой ***в одну игру*** **будем** ***очень интересную*** **играть //**
(Лап 1965:15) Сейчас мы с тобой будем играть в одну очень интересную игру.
You and I are now going to play a very interesting game.

Independent Clause Separated by Independent Clause

Выключи / ***комары летят*** **/ свет-то //**
(Зем 1973:331) Выключи свет-то. Комары летят.
Turn off the light; (because) mosquitos are coming in.

Ручку / ***магазин открылся недавно*** **/ я купил //**
(Шир 1970:168) Я купил ручку в магазине, (который) недавно открылся.
I bought a pen in a store that opened recently.

In both examples we can see also the absence of a connector. In the example *Выключи свет-то, [потому что] комары летят* the KLJ version can actually be thought of as two complete utterances/sentences. Adding a connector actually results in one clause becoming dependent.

Мы/***квартира большая у них*** **/ часто останавливаемся //**
(Зем 1973:334) Мы часто останавливаемся, [потому что] у них большая квартира.
We often stop over [because] they have a large apartment.

<u>Сломался</u> / *ничего теперь не сделаешь* / <u>твой автомобиль</u>//

(Зем 1973:333) Сломался твой автомобиль, [так] ничего теперь не сделаешь.

Your car broke down [so] now there's nothing you can do.

<u>Я психологически как-то не мог</u> / *была возможность* / <u>с ней встретиться</u> //

(Зем 1973:331) Я психологически как-то не мог с ней встретиться, [хотя] была возможность.

Psychologically, I just couldn't meet her [although] there was an opportunity.

<u>Чашки</u> *я ему подарить собираюсь* <u>красивые</u> //

(Зем 1987:153) Чашки, которые я собираюсь ему подарить красивые //

The cups I plan to give him look great.

Independent Clause Separated by Dependent Clause

In KLJ, even when an independent clause is interrupted by a dependent clause, the placing of the subordinating connector allows for no variation. As stated above, the subordinating connector must precede the dependent clause. In CR, as you'll see from the examples below, the placement of these connectors is quite free.

This type of construction differs from the standard separation of an independent clause by a dependent *который* clause *(человек / который живет здесь / очень любит музыку //*) in that, unlike the connector *который*, the ones in this construction type either may occur in the initial position or play no part in the dependent clause itself. For example, in *который живет*, *который* is the subject of the clause. Each dependent clause below has its own basic constituents and, therefore, the effect is similar to that of the separation of one independent clause by another:

<u>Очень</u> / *когда цветов много* стоит / <u>нарядно</u> у вас //

(Зем 1971:17) Когда цветов много стоит, очень нарядно у вас.

When all the flowers are up, it looks very decorative at your place.

Было еще / ***когда я проснулся*** / **рано очень** //
(Зем 1971:17) Когда я проснулся, было очень рано.
It was still very early when I woke up.

Они ушли уже / ***когда он приехал*** / **в кино** //
(Зем 1971:17) Когда он приехал, они уже ушли в кино.
When he arrived, they had already left for the movies.

Люся не пойдет / ***если будет дождь*** / **в лес** //
(Зем 1971:17) Если будет дождь, Люся не пойдет в лес.
Lyusya won't go to the woods if it rains.

Иванову / ***что в библиотеке ремонт*** / **сообщили** //
(Зем 1971:17) Иванову сообщили, что в библиотеке ремонт.
Ivanov was informed that they're making repairs in the library.

Dependent Clause Separated by Independent Clause

In this construction type, the independent clause comes armed with the subordinating connector. In this example, the utterance begins with the subject of the dependent clause:

Петров / ***странно что*** **нам помогал** //
(Зем 1971:15) Странно, что Петров нам помогал.
It's strange that Petrov helped us.

Verbs of reporting—said, heard, wrote, etc—are very often used:

Богачева мать / ***все говорят что*** **красивая** //
(Зем 1971:15) Все говорят, что мать Богачева красивая.
Everyone says Bogachyov's mom is pretty.

Моего сына первая жена / ***ему рассказывали*** /**что докторскую защитила** // (Зем 1973:399) Ему рассказывали, что первая жена моего сына защитила докторскую диссертацию.
They told him that my son's first wife successfully defended her doctoral dissertation.

In the following examples, the object of the dependent clause begins the utterance:

Direct object

Носки / ***я рада*** **что купила** //
(Зем 1971:14) Я рада, что купила носки.
I'm glad I bought socks.

Посылку ***видели*** / **как запаковали?**
(Зем 1971:15) Видели, как запаковали посылку?
Did you see how they packed the package?

Object-destination

В Ленинград ***сказали / что*** **командируют** //
(Зем 1971:15) Сказали, что [их] командируют в Ленинград.
They said that [they] are being sent to Leningrad.

Никуда ***я плохо себя чувствую*** **не пойду** //
(Зем 1981:246) Я никуда не пойду потому, что я плохо себя чувствую.
I'm not feeling well [so] won't be going anywhere.

Interspersing of Two Clauses

Finally, some utterances in CR can be characterized as being 'mixtures' of two clauses. That is, neither clause is continuous. The utterance is usually complex (one independent and one dependent clause). Very often this construction is accompanied also by inversion of, what would be in KLJ, normal word order:

Катю / ***ты*** **за что исключили** / ***догадалась*?**
(Зем 1971:16) Ты догадалась, за что исключили Катю?
Have you guessed why Katya was expelled?

Мне тоже / ***Ирина*** **нравится** / ***как пишет*** //
(Зем 1971:16) Мне тоже нравится, как Ирина пишет.
I too like the way Irina writes.

Мам / знаешь ***мне очень*** **<u>какая</u>** ***понравилась*** **/ <u>картина</u>**
(Лап 1976:238) Мам, знаешь какая картина мне очень понравилась?
Mom, know which picture I really liked?

UNUSUAL PLACEMENT OF SUBORDINATING CONNECTORS

In some of the above examples, the unusual placement of subordinating connectors may have already been noticed by the reader. Since the focus was at the time on the clauses themselves, the connectors were not mentioned. Placement of subordinating connectors in CR may be quite varied. As shown above, they may even be deleted altogether. Zemskaya provides these examples of some variations:

Потому что

1. Все устали **потому что** было жарко.
2. Все устали было жарко **потому что.**
3. Все устали было **потому что** жарко.
4. Все устали жарко **потому что** было.
5. **Потому что** было жарко все устали.
6. Было жарко **потому что /** все устали.
7. Жарко **потому что** было / все устали.
8. Было **потому что жарко /** все устали.

Everyone was tired because it was hot.

Если

1. Мы в кино не успеем / **если** он придет поздно.
2. **Если** он придет поздно / мы в кино не успеем.
3. Мы в кино не успеем / он придет поздно **если.**
4. Мы в кино не успеем / он **если** придет поздно.
5. Он **если** придет поздно / мы в кино не успеем.

If he comes late, we won’t make it to the show in time.

Что

1. Ты доволен **что** сын приехал?
2. Ты доволен сын **что** приехал**?**
3. Ты доволен приехал **что** сын**?**
4. **Что** приехал сын ты доволен?
5. Сын **что** приехал ты доволен?
6. Приехал **что** сын ты доволен?
   (Зсм 1973:396-97)
   Are you happy/satisfied that your son came?

Below are some CR examples with a KLJ version and a translation:

<u>Потому что / из-за того, что</u>

Саша не мог приехать / дождь потому что //
(Зем 1987:159) …потому что был/шел дождь
Sasha couldn't come because of the rain.

Холодно ветер потому что //
(Зем 1981:232) Холодно из-за ветра
The wind's making it cold.

Я одна дома / Миша потому что в Крым уехал //
(Зем 1987:159) …потому что Миша уехал в Крым
I'm by myself because Misha went to the Crimea.

Сегодня они не учатся / воскресенье потому что //
(Лап 1976: 200) Не учатся, потому что сегодня воскресенье.
Today they're not in school because it's Sunday.

<u>Если</u>

Неприятно / дождь пойдет если //
(Зем 1973:394) Будет неприятно, если дождь пойдет.
It would be unpleasant if it rains.

Да брось ты // ну не хочет он если //
(Лап 1976:318) Да брось ты, если он не хочет.
Hey, forget it, if he doesn't want to.

Ну не понимает человек если / что можно ему говорить?
(Лап 1976:318) Ну если человек не понимает,…
Well, if a person doesn't understand, what can you tell him?

Спать захочешь если / спи в удобном кресле //
(Лап 1976:204) Если хочешь спать…
If you want to sleep, sleep in a comfortable armchair.

Вот они на дачу поедут если / там и встретитесь //
(Зем 1987:159) Если они на дачу поедут…
Now if they go to the dacha, you can meet them there.

Когда

И вчера был снег вечером / я шла когда //
(Лап 1976:317) И вчера был снег вечером, когда я шла.
Last evening also it was snowing when I was walking.

Я позвонил вам когда / никто не ответил //
(Зем 1973:394) Когда я позвонил вам, никто не ответил.
When I called you, no one answered.

Вот я когда туда приехал /…
(Лап 1976:298) Вот когда я туда приехал…
When I got there…

Который

Т. / где у вас который кофе в пакетиках?
(Лап 1966:52) … кофе, который в пакетиках?
Where's your coffee that's in little packets?

А где карандаш Иван Иваныч подарил который?
(Лап 1976:301 … карандаш, который Иван Иваныч подарил…
Where's the pencil Ivan Ivanovich gave as a gift?

Надень кофту там висит которая //
(Лап 1976:301) … кофту, которая там висит
Put on the cardigan that's hanging there.

Где

Ты был / новую школу где строят?
(Зем 1973:396) Ты был, где строят новую школу?
Have you been where they're building a new school?

Не знаешь / полотенце где?
(Зем 1973:394) Не знаешь, где полотенце?
You know where the towel is?

Что

Он звонил придет что
(Зем 1981:232) Он звонил, что…
He called and said he'd come.

-Ну он через полчаса будет?
-Минут через сорок надеюсь что//
(Лап 1976:199) Надеюсь, что минут через сорок
- Will he be here in half and hour?
- In about 40 minutes, I hope.

- Мне нельзя пить //
- За рулем из-за того что?
(Лап 1976:199) Из-за того что за рулем?
-I can't have anything to drink.
-Because you're driving?

Чтобы

Я вешалку принесла / повесить чтобы //
(Зем 1973:394) Я принесла вешалку, чтобы повесить [что-то].
I brought a hanger to hang [something].

Я тетрадь взяла записывать чтобы //
(Зем 1976:394) чтобы записывать
I took the notebook to make notes.

Prepositions

In CR double prepositions may be used:

Ты оставь конфету на после сна //
(Зем 1983:96)
Leave that candy until after you sleep.

Можешь взять книгу до после каникул //
(Зем 1983:96)
You can take the book until after the holidays.

SUMMARY OF WORD ORDER

As stated above, in CR word order, the conscious motivating factor is the speaker's emphasis. Furthermore, the fact that CR is not rehearsed also plays an important role in the way an utterance develops. Reduced to writing, a colloquial utterance with unusual word order can probably be decoded by the student, especially if he or she has been made aware of the more recurring emphasis-determined construction types. Although mixture of clauses may initially cause confusion, in CR word order the syntactic relationships usually are consistent. In live speech, he or she must, in addition, be capable of discriminating emphasis-determined intonation patterns (logical stress). The most important point to be made in this chapter, however, is that what seems at first glance to be arbitrary word ordering in CR can be explained with definite, describable patterned phenomena.

CHAPTER 8

Vocabulary

GENERAL CHARACTERISTICS OF CR VOCABULARY

Vocabulary is the most dynamic element in any language. New technology, political and social developments, mass media and contact with foreign cultures give rise to words that at first start as neologisms.[107] Some of these words will find their way into the standard, codified language. Many such words begin in CR, but both CR and KLJ are recipients of new developments in a language's lexicon.

The CR lexicon is more than just words. It contains phenomena that are typical of CR, but not KLJ. For example, many words are absent/deleted in CR utterances, but communication is still possible because of extra-linguistic factors—*конситуация*. A very wide range of vocabulary is possible, but this *конситуация*—direct contact, gestures, the object itself, the speaker's personal attitude toward the object in question, shared knowledge of the subject, a speaker's personality and favorite words or phrases in speech—makes conversation intelligible.

At first glance, CR vocabulary seems haphazard and limitless in its range. In some respects, it *is* limitless since the variety of subjects found in CR is immense. V.D. Devkin states: "Strictly speaking, topical or thematic boundaries are not fixed in CR. One may speak of politics, economic, scientific or technical matters or on general cultural themes: art, literature, music, education."[108]

There are, however, certain words and patterns in CR that can be presented in the Russian language classroom.

Although the basic form of CR is oral speech, colloquial elements have found their way, more and more, into written form. This is an important aspect of modern Russian literature and mass media. Additionally, the written form is the way most students may first come into contact with CR.

DICTIONARIES

Before we explore the phenomena and patterns in colloquial vocabulary, a word about the notation *разг* (colloquial) in Russian dictionaries. Denisov and Kostomarov point to the caution needed when identifying CR words from standard dictionaries. Their research was based on words found in Ozhegov's dictionary.[109]

First of all, the words listed as colloquial in his dictionary are taken from literary texts or what the Russians call "stylized colloquial speech." Second, many words listed as "colloquial" in dictionaries are accompanied by other stylistic notes such as "specialized," "official," "sub-standard," "bookish," "high style," "derogatory," "ironic," "joking," etc. Anyone who has looked up the meaning of a word in a dictionary is well aware that many meanings are often given, which can be confusing. Consequently, it is difficult to isolate the meaning one is after. How then does one select the appropriate word?[110] Sometimes only by the context, if we know it.

Ozhegov uses 15 different notes to characterize word styles—from colloquial to archaic. Of the 17,003 notes he attaches to words and phrases in his dictionary, 5,768 are listed as "colloquial" (3,225 of which pertain to single words). Furthermore, for many of these words the term "colloquial" is accompanied by several other notes, e.g., "ancient,"" "unacceptable," "ironic," "humorous," etc.[111]

The fact is, however, many of Ozhegov's colloquial words were seldom found in live, recorded CR. According to O.B. Sirotinina, some words were not found at all. In the *2380 наиболее употребительных слов в русской разговорной речи*, only 17 of Ozhegov's colloquial words were listed: ***парень, видно, немножко, девчонка, дочка, мальчишка, пятерка, картошка, неделька, бумажка, бабка, минутка, ей-богу, вовсе, рыбалка, ишь*** and ***ребятишки***, most of which don't occur in the top 1,000 words in that list.[112]

WORD FREQUENCY LISTS

Since research on CR began to intensify in the 1950s and 1960s, the publication of a series of frequency word lists offered a step forward in identifying CR vocabulary. N.P. Vakar's *Word Count of Spoken Russian* (1966) was one of the first publications to highlight words in what we might now call CR. His list, however, was based exclusively on his own analysis of 93 Soviet dramas. Although limited by his choice of sources, this was a major pioneering effort, motivated by the belief, as he writes on the first page:

> Whatever the theory and method of instruction, the initial selection of words and sentence structures is the first problem the teacher and the student of any foreign language must face. In fact, the vocabulary selection largely determines the content and organization of a language manual for beginners.[113]

In a comprehensive review of all earlier attempts to identify useable word lists, Vakar points to serious discrepancies between the earlier word counts compiled by H.H. Josselson and E.A. Shteinfeldt.[114] In those works only 35 words are common to the top 100 of both lists. Vakar quite correctly notes that "the disparity in basic vocabularies for different types of discourse is, indeed, greater than it is commonly believed to be."

Apparently not available at that time, or unknown to Vakar (and to his reviewer in 1967) was a Soviet list based on live recordings of colloquial speech, which had been published in *Русский язык в национальной школе* in 1965.[115] Here Yu. Markov and T. Vishnyakova presented 1200 words from 234 live conversations recorded in Moscow. The 155 informants ranged widely in age and occupation, but most had more than a high-school education. The most significant feature of a word on the list was its use in many different conversations, since it was possible that some individuals might have a propensity to use a particular word uncommonly often. The publication of this article marked the beginning of extensive statistical research and theoretical discussions on the methods and reliability of frequency lists, as well as their value to vocabulary 'minimums.'[116]

The years 1965-1971 saw the publication of numerous studies on Russian vocabulary, both standard and specialized. In a 1972 publication, *Лексические минимумы русского языка*, one finds an excellent summary of most of the work to that date. Unfortunately, it's a volume that isn't readily available in this country.

Not included in *Лексические минимумы...* are the articles devoted to CR vocabulary peculiarities found in RRR-70. RRR-73 and RRR-87 present statistical studies of various classes of words. For example, scholars studied the frequency of nouns in CR—including a breakdown of case frequency. Earlier, in 1968, a new and more comprehensive frequency list was published—*2380 наиболее...* (Referred to above*)*. Thereafter, this list became the reference source for many vocabulary studies.

Even though frequency lists based on live, recorded speech are useful, there are some differences between the lists, primarily due to the differences in the corpuses studied. The word *быть*, for example, was the most frequently used word in *2380 наиболее...*, although it was fourth in a study by T.A. Vasilenko and T.I. Koltsova. Verbs of speech (e.g., *говорить, сказать*) placed second on both lists. Vasilenko and Koltsova's corpus showed verbs of motion the most used, although they came up 9th and 12th in other frequency lists.[117]

Although all frequency lists are valuable in the study of CR, there are some drawbacks to using them for the classroom. Some important words are not of high frequency. Household terms, for example, seldom rank high on frequency lists. Nevertheless, these words are useful for the student's ability to participate in household conversations. Such words are:

чайник - teapot
солонка - salt shaker
сковородка - frying pan
ложка - spoon
тарелка - plate
умывальник - sink
гребешок - comb
тряпка - rag
щетка – brush
кастрюля - sauce pan
плита - stove
вилка - fork
блюдце - saucer
чашка - cup
расческа - comb
заколка – hairpin/barrette
(Зем 1987:32)

A couple of these words (*вилка, блюдце*) don't show up at all on the *2380 наиболее...* list.[118]

Some colloquial words used for money may be substituted for the normal terms. These too are absent from such lists:

две копейки > **двушка**	two kopecks
пять копеек > **пятак, пятачок**	five kopecks
три рубля > **трешка, трешница, трояк**	three rubles
пять рублей > **пятёрка**	five rubles
десять рублей > **десятка**	ten rubles
сто рублей > **сотня, сотенная, сотняга**	one hundred rubles

(Зем 1987:33)

Even old terms for money may be substituted:

десять копеек > **гривенник**	ten kopecks
двадцать копеек > **двугривенный**	twenty kopecks
один рубль > **целковый**	one ruble

(Зем 1987:34)

INTRODUCTORY WORDS

The most frequent introductory words and phrases in CR are:

значит	that means
вообще	in general, generally
в общем	in general, generally
например	for example
во-первых	in the first place
между прочим	by the way
наоборот	just the opposite
тем не менее	nevertheless
таким образом	in such a way

(Коз/Гус, 1970:117)

Other frequent words include:

конечно	of course
возможно	it's possible
правда	true
надо полагать	one has to assume
буквально	literally
может быть	maybe
может	maybe
действительно	actually
кажется	it seems
во всяком случае	in any case
наверно	probably

впрямь	directly
чувствуется	one gets the feeling
(Коз/Гус, 1970:117)	

SHARED WORDS IN CR AND KLJ

KLJ and CR share many words, which is understandable since both versions are part of the overall Russian language. Often there is no difference whether a word is from CR or KLJ. If so, it is considered neutral. For example, in the *2380 наиболее...* list, the following adjectives had high frequency:

хороший	good
большой	large, big
новый	new
красивый	pretty, beautiful
добрый	kind, good
плохой	bad
маленький	small, little
старый	old
многий	many
(Зем 1987:34)	

These words are also frequent in KLJ.

Some words, on the other hand, have different meanings in KLJ and CR. A good example of this is the word *нормальный* and its adverb *нормально.* According to most dictionaries, the KLJ word is defined as "usual, not deviating from the norm." In CR, however, the word is used much more widely and indicates that something is good, fine or ok:

Как твоя голова? Не болит?
Нормально //
(Зем 1987:37)

How's your head? Ache?
It's fine.

Как живешь?
Нормально //
(Зем 1987:37)

How's it going?
Fine.

Удачно съездили?
Нормально//
(Зем 1987:37)

You make it ok?
Yeah, all went well.

Хорошее здесь дно?
Нормально // песчаное //
(Зем 1987:37)

Is the bottom good?
Good. Sandy.

Some older Russians may object to this usage even though it's quite widespread today. Zemskaya presents this dialogue between a young girl and her grandmother:

- **Люба, как у тебя с письменным заданием по литературе? - спросила бабушка.**
- **Нормально, - ответила Люба, глядя на себя в зеркало.**
- **Что значит «нормально»? Неужели нельзя ответить по-человечески?**
- **Бабуленька, - сказала Люба, поправляя волосы, - когда тебя спрашивают, как ты себя чувствуешь, ты отвечаешь: «ничего». Ты что, думаешь, в твоем ответе больше информации?**
(Зем 1987:37fn)

"Lyuba, how's your written assignment in literature going?" asked the grandmother.
"[Normal] Fine," answered Lyuba, looking at herself in the mirror.
"What does 'normal' mean? Can't you answer like a human?"
"Granny," said Lyuba, fixing her hair, "when someone asks you how you feel, you answer 'it's nothing.' So, what do you think, is there more information in your answer?"

The following dialogue provides a clear contrast between the use of a CR phrase and one in KLJ:

(Three men stand at a bus stop in Moscow)
A: (Looking up the street) **Длинная коробочка идет//**
B: (Politely) **Вы имеете в виду автобус повышенной вместимости?**
C: Ну / знаете / в часы пик у всех автобусов повышенная вместимость //
(Зем 1987:49)

A. A long box is coming.
B. You mean a bus with increased capacity?
C. Well, you know, during rush hour all busses have increased capacity.

Here both the KLJ and CR descriptions of the bus are given—the colloquial *длинная коробочка* is used to denote the official KLJ *автобус повышенной вместимости.*

FIGURATIVE MEANINGS OF SELECT WORDS

Some words in CR can take on figurative meanings, most often negative. They are particularly frequent in words based on food, but are completely dissociated from the food item itself, having only the figurative meaning seen below:

	Meaning in KLJ	Meaning in CR
винегрет	salad medley	a mixture of diverse items
каша	kasha	mix-up, lack of order
лапша	noodles	mix-up, indecisive person
размазня	thin porridge	wishy-washy, indecisive person
перец	pepper	to really give it to someone
конфетка	candy	something pretty, pleasant
сапог	boot	vulgar person, someone who doesn't understand something
кукла	doll	soulless, lifeless [woman]
юла	spinning top	fidget
резина	rubber	something stretchable, not approved
ртуть	chemical mercury	fast learner, high achiever

(Зем 1987:43)

ECONOMY OF SPEECH

Economy of speech is a primary characteristic of CR. Mark T. Hooker calls this the Law of the Conservation of Linguistic Energy. It can be achieved in many ways, as can be seen above. In some cases, the situational context is absolutely obligatory in order to understand the utterance. Given the situation, it is often unnecessary to provide a full descriptions of people or objects. For the examples below, the explanations are provided by Zemskaya.

In a store:
Десять в клеточку / три в линеечку //
(о тетрадях, которые лежат на прилавке)
(Зем 1987:51)
I'll take ten graph-paper notebooks and three with lined pages.

У Катеньки температура //
(возвышенная температура)
(Зем 1987:64)
Katenka has a temperature (Same as in English.)

У тебя давление / да?
(возвышенное давление)
(Зем 1987:64)
Do you have high blood pressure?

Ивана Петровича сняли //
(с работы)
(Зем 1987:65)
They fired Ivan Petrovich?

Economy of speech is also achieved by shortening a phrase or adding different meanings to a word to identify a person or object. For example, the naming of a nationality may mean something other than just a nationality:

У вас француженка новенькая?
(Зем 1987:51)
Do you have a new French teacher?

Завтра они на итальянцев идут //
(Зем 1987:51fn)
Tomorrow they're going to see an Italian film.

HYPERBOLE

Hyperbole is another phenomenon in CR—as it is in the colloquial speech of most languages. These words are used to show extreme expressiveness:

В каждом вагоне чистота <u>бешеная</u> //
(Зем 1987:43)
Every car was insanely clean.

Пить хочется! <u>Умереть</u> //
(Зем 1987:43)
I'm dying of thirst.

Я тебе этих яблок привезу <u>вагон</u> / сколько хочешь //
(Зем 1987:43)
I'll bring you a whole carload of the apples. As many as you want.

У них <u>гора</u> цветов / не знают куда ставить //
(Зем 1987:43)
They have a mountain of flowers. They don't know where to put them.

Котлеты вышли <u>асфальтовые</u> //
(Зем 1981:47)
The cutlets turned out like asphalt.

COMPREHENSIVE DEFINING DICTIONARY (*ТОЛКОВЫЙ СЛОВАРЬ…*)

To the good fortune of all CR scholars, a new publication has appeared that comprehensibly describes much CR vocabulary. Edited by L.P. Krysin, this multi-volume work is *Толковый словарь русской разговорной речи.* The dictionary (published in four volumes so far) represents a major contribution to the study of CR.[119] It contains only words that have been observed in CR and the only definitions given are the ones that apply to CR.

This dictionary, unlike all standard ones and frequency lists, provides colloquial definitions, linguistic and social categories, and examples of usage for each entry. It also presents many words that are not found on any frequency lists. The dictionary includes words from recordings of live oral conversations, from contemporary literature, public speeches, the press, television, radio, dramatic scripts, jargon, slang, and various Internet sources (blogs, forums, chat rooms, etc). Krysin justifies taking words from these sources because, as he notes:

> Linguists write of the never-before-seen and uncharacteristic Russian language colloquialization in the public sphere of communication (that is, the plethora there of colloquial elements). (Крыс 2008:111)

In fact, this dictionary contains many words that aren't, strictly speaking, acceptable as proper such as jargon, substandard, obscenities, etc. Krysin, however, identifies such words in this dictionary with the terms *сниженный, отрицательный, грубый* (lower style, negative or rude). All entries, however, are words actually noted in the conversational speech of what Krysin calls the Russian 'intelligentsia.'

The range for the corpus used in the dictionary is thus much wider than the one other scholars have used and on which we've based our examples in this book. Many of the words in this dictionary are low frequency.

Depending on the number of definitions and illustrative examples for an entry, some of the articles are short, but others are long. *Минутка*, for example, has three pages devoted to it, while *мозги* takes up six pages and *нос* takes three and a half pages. The dictionary entry for *пойти* has eight definitions and phrases used in CR; it stretches to three and a half pages. The word *рука* has only one definition but the number of its phrases takes over fifteen pages. All this clearly illustrates the breadth of vocabulary in CR.

Examples: [with my translations, jrh]:

ВОДА (Крыс 2008)[120]

Definition 1: Basin/reservoir for swimming.

У вас на даче вода есть, где купаться?

Do you have a swimming pool at the dacha?

Definition 2. Water supply system.

Им еще воду не подвели.

They haven't connected them to a [running] water system yet.

Morphology: no plural.

Definition 3: Figurative. Wordiness without useful content.

В докладе одна вода.

That was a useless report.

Morphology: no plural.

Phrase: лить воду. Talk for a long time without useful content.

Хватит воду лить - скажи, чего тебе надо.

Enough drivel, tell me what you need.

ГДЕ-НИБУДЬ (ТолкСлов 2014:300)

Definition 1: An approximate time, not clearly defined.

Зайдите где-нибудь в пол-десятого.

Come by sometime around 9:30.

Synonym: что-нибудь.

Phonetic: In rapid speech pronounced like [гден'т'].

Definition 2: An approximate number or quantity of something.

Мы теряем на этом где-нибудь процентов десять.

We lose somewhere around ten percent on that.

Synonyms: что-нибудь, что-то.

Here is an example taken from the nearly three pages devoted to the word *куда* and its many illustrative examples:

КУДА (ТолкСлов 2017:150)

Definition 4: much more (намного, гораздо).

Карточка / она куда удобнее / деньги не надо носить//

A [credit] card is a lot more convenient. One doesn't have to carry money.

У вас положение куда хуже моего //

Your situation is a lot worse than mine.

Morphology: Adverb.

Syntax: Used together with comparative forms.

Style: Lower, familiar. [Disagree about 'lower.' This is used widely in normal conversational Russian. jrh]

Some other examples:

МЫЛО (ТолкСлов 2020:368)

Definition: Electronic address, electronic mail.

Слушай / скинь мне на мыло что /куда /когда//А то я забуду сразу //

Listen, send me an e-mail indicating what, where and when. Otherwise, I'll forget it immediately.

Ну давай / я тебе по мылу напишу / все / пока //

So, I'll send you an e-mail, that's all, bye.

Надо дать должное нашему языковому чутью / сделать из измейла два русских слова «мыло» и «емеля». Это красиво / согласитесь //

One has to give credit to our language sense. To make two Russian words «мыло» and «емеля». That's cool, [you] have to agree.

Morphology: Neuter, no plural.

Style: Computer

Synonym: Емеля

Pragmatics: Arose because it sounded similar to the English word 'e-mail.'

ЧТО-ТО (Крыс 2008)

Definition: About an approximate number, amount of something.

Их было что-то человек десять-двенадцать.

They were somewhere around ten-twelve people.

Что-то около тонны осталось.

Something around a ton remained.

Synonyms: где-нибудь, что-нибудь.

Phonetics: In rapid speech is pronounced as [шотъ], [чётъ].

PARTICLES

Particles (*частицы)* are interesting vocabulary items. They are very frequent in CR. In scientific Russian, for example, particles are used 1.6 percent of the time, while in CR that percentage increases to 11.6.[121] In CR they are used in dialogue responses, for emphasis and expressiveness, as well as fillers when a person is searching for a word. Their primary role is that of emotional expression. All persons, regardless of age, profession or level of education, use these particles.

The difficulty with describing particles is that most of them have no intrinsic meaning, or perhaps it's better to say they can have many meanings, depending how they are used. They are not to be found in the Krysin's *Толковый словарь*.

Many particles are almost synonymous—several examples exist where one or the other carries similar meaning. Since they are so frequent in CR, a short summary of their usages is provided here. For a more detailed description of particles, see the easily available book (in English) by Vasilyeva: *Particles in Colloquial Russian*. She has hundreds of examples and shows how some particles can be replaced by others.[122] A few of her explanations and examples are provided below (all are taken from her book).

ВЕДЬ—comes from the verb *ведать* (to know) and carries the idea of an argument requiring no proof. The vowel is always unstressed:

Ведь иначе и быть не может.

It just couldn't be any other way.

ЖЕ—categoric and insistent emphasis of the indisputability of a fact. Although carrying a similar meaning to *ведь*, it's much stronger. It's usually placed after the word being stressed. When used with an imperative or instruction, it differs from *ведь* and generally reflects insistence, irritation, impatience or perhaps refusal. The particle is always unstressed and sometimes the vowel is deleted (*же* > *ж*):

У тебя же температура!

You have a temperature, after all!

-ТО—This particle, like so many others, is also used to emphasize or stress something. It comes from the demonstrative pronoun *том*. It contrasts with *ведь* and *же* in that it emphasizes the speaker's wish to highlight something, rather than to express an emotional connotation to an utterance. *-то* usually emphasizes a single word. The contrast can be seen in this exchange:

От работы мы не отказываемся, но о человеке больше надо заботиться. Люди-то живые…

It's not that we're refusing to work, but one should show more consideration for people. People aren't machines after all…

In the last phrase, if *Люди ведь живые* were used, the meaning would be more like 'And you should have known that,' or 'you could have guessed it yourself.'

Other examples:

Какая тишина-то!
Oh, how wonderfully quiet!

- В кино идете?
- Пошли, да вернулись. Билетов-то не было.
You going to the movies?
We went, but we're back. All the tickets were sold out.

УЖ—This particle obviously comes from the adverb *уже*. It suggests the incontrovertibility of something or the impossibility of changing something. In contrasting *уж* to *-то, уж* merely expresses certainty, while *-то* tends rather to emphasize something:

- Пойдешь с работы, зайди в аптеку.
- Уж обязательно.
When you leave work, stop by the pharmacy.
Yes, for sure.

Не хвались уж, мог бы и получше сделать.
Stop boasting. You could have done better still.

ВОТ, ВОН have many meanings, depending on the word(s) they're emphasizing. This may be location, a whole phrase or a complete utterance. It sometimes is synonymous with *же* and *-то*:

Вот правильно!
That's exactly right!

Вот красота!
Now that's pretty!

НУ in its neutral usage means 'well.' It can, however, take on several other meanings, just as 'well' can in English:

> **Ну как вы тут? Живы-здоровы?**
>
> So how are you? Alive and kicking?

> **Ну, что скажешь?**
>
> Well, what do you say [to that]?

КА is used as a gentle, familiar exhortation. It is usually used with imperatives. It is sometimes used also with first person singular when the speaker is debating with him or herself what to do. Vasilyeva describes that as "When a person is thinking aloud."

> **Дай-ка мне рублей десять. Может, на обратном пути забегу в магазин.**
>
> Let me have about ten rubles. I might stop at the store on the way back.

> **Займусь-ка я репетицией перед зеркалом…А может, лучше погулять?**
>
> I might practice in front of the mirror…Or maybe it would be better to go for a walk.

ТАК in its neutral meaning means 'so.' In CR it can show emphasis on cause and effect—a connection to the preceding utterance, or the result of an agreement. In many cases, one can think of this particle as simply English 'so.'

> **Замечательное приспособление! Так это вы его придумали?**
>
> What a great device! So it was you who thought it up, right?

> **А пришла на лекцию—так сиди, слушай, другим не мешай.**
>
> Once you're at a lecture, sit quietly, listen and don't disturb anyone.

ЕЩЕ can have many meanings, as seen from the examples below:

Он меня еще учит жизни!
And he still dares tell me how to live my life!

А еще инженер!
And an engineer at that!
Cf. also: **Уж инженер!**
Ну инженер!
Вот инженер!

- Ну, наелись?
- Еще как наелись! На три дня вперед!
Did you have enough to eat?
Enough? We won't need another meal for three days!

Я, может, еще приду.
Maybe I'll still come.

- Я хочу научиться прыгать с парашютом.
- Еще чего вздумал! Ты с ума сошел!
I want to learn to jump with a parachute.
What'll you think of next? You must be mad!

И—This particle is used for emphasis of a word or action and is sometimes synonymous with *даже* or with other particles indicating certainty. It usually precedes the word or phrase being emphasized:

- Нет, ты молчи, ты мне ничего не говори.
- Я ничего и не говорю.
Now don't you talk back, don't say anything to me.
But I haven't said anything.

Тогда мы и познакомились.
It was then that we indeed did meet.

- Может быть, встречались мы с вами где-нибудь?
- Может, и встречались.

Perhaps we've met somewhere?
Maybe so.

ДА—Another particle used for emphasis of the next word or phrase:

Да не может быть!

But that's impossible!

- С каким артистом ходит?
- Да не знаю.

Which actor is [she] going around with?
No idea.[123]

А—In KLJ this is generally used as an interjection or as a conjunction meaning 'but.' As a particle it may be used in CR when the speaker is making a request or looking for an answer:

Нет ли мне писем, а?

Any letters for me?

Яблоко дать, а?

Would you like an apple?

ХОТЬ, ХОТЯ—This particle often translates into English as 'even' or 'for example.'

Кто из вас перенес войны, хоть одну, тот знает какие ужасы…

Those of you who have lived through wars, even one, know what horrors they reveal…

При работе важно, какую позу занимает человек. Взять хоть тебя…

When working, it's important to pay attention to your posture. Take you, for example…

ЛИ is an interrogative in KLJ that generally means 'whether.' As a particle it connotates alternative, doubt or uncertainty. It's sometimes combined with *что*:

Не случилось ли чего?
Has something happened?

Не Федор ли там?
Is that Fyodor there?

Врача, что ли, вызвать?
Should I call a doctor, or what?

ЧТО—This particle derives from the pronoun *что*. It emphasizes a question, a disagreement or a statement of the opposite:

Что, отец не приходил еще?
So, your dad hasn't come yet?
Cf. also: **Отец-то не приходил еще?**

Ты что, с ума сошла?
Are you mad or what?

- Советую не ездить на север. Там такой холод.
- Что холод! Я к холодам с детства привык.
- I advise you not to go north. It's so cold there.
- Cold's nothing. I've been used to cold since I was a kid.

NOMINATION

Whereas in KLJ the subject or object is usually a noun or pronoun, in CR they can be replaced by various expressions. The replacement/substitution of a phrase that clearly indicates what noun is needed is called nomination (*номинация*). These nominations will not be found in a dictionary, so the student should familiarize him- or herself with this phenomenon.

It's important to reiterate the importance of the situational context in order to understand how CR can differ so from KLJ and still be considered acceptable to educated Russians. The *конситуация* is a full-fledged constituent of almost all uses of CR, something that is duly emphasized by scholars. It's almost, as Michelle Berdy writes, "…in Russian context is everything."[124] Given the face-to-face contact, shared knowledge of the subject and the presumed need to be as brief as possible, many conversations are abbreviated. Gestures also play an important role. Nomination suggests the noun(s) that is/are being replaced.

An adjective with an unstated noun, for example, can mean many things. Here the situation must be known to identify what the utterance means. In such cases, of which there are many in CR, the naming device may not be understood without knowledge of the situation. For example, the meaning of the word *тарахтелка* by itself, means very little, except that it denotes something that makes unpleasant noise. In the context of a man standing on the beach and watching boats go by saying:

> **Опять эти <u>тарахтелки</u> покоя не дадут.**
> (Зем 1987:51)
>
> Again those noisemakers are disturbing the peace.
> (The meaning becomes clear.)

Adjectives

Adjectives, in particular, are often used to identify the noun(s) referred to. Here are examples of the most frequent categories of adjectives that may replace nouns:

About people—where they live, kind of work or study: ***интститутские, заводские, университетские, школьные, факультетские*** *и т.д.* (люди)

About types of food: ***сладкое, молочное, первое, второе, мясное, рыбное, горячее*** *(блюда)*

About clothing: ***зимнее, летнее, теплое, шерстяное, праздничное*** *(платье)*

About various vacations: ***двухмеячный, двухгодичный, академический*** *(отпуск)*

About medicines: ***снотроное, слабительное*** *(лекарство)*

About meetings: ***профсоюзное, открытое*** **(***собрание***)**

About examinations: ***выпускные, вступительные, государственные*** *(экзамены)*

About departments in a college: ***классическое, славянское, русское*** *(отделение)*

About work or residence: ***заводские, рязанские*** (люди) (Зем 1987: 63-64)

Examples:

У них <u>мясного</u> и детям не дают //
(Зем 1973:414)
They don't give even the children meat dishes.

Не люблю <u>соленого</u> //
(Зем 1973:414)
I don't like anything that's salty.

Наши <u>университетские</u> не знали про ваше заседание //
(Зем 1973:413)
Our university faculty/students didn't know about your meeting.

Наши <u>заводские</u> только в этой столовой обедают //
(Зем 1973:413)
Our factory workers eat only in this dining hall.

Я <u>заграничного</u> не ношу / неохота бегать доставать // (Зем 1973:413)
I can't stand foreign goods. I don't want to chase around to get them.

Descriptive Phrases

Descriptive phrases that refer to an unstated noun are often used in CR. As with individual adjectives, a phrase that describes a location, what one wears or looks like, or what one does can be substituted for a noun subject or object.

Examples as subject:

<u>**С зелеными балконами**</u> **/ это ваш?**
(Зем 1973:227)
The place with the green balconies, is that yours?

<u>**Молоко разносит**</u> **/ не приходила еще?**
(Зем 1973:227)
Has the woman who delivers milk arrived yet?

<u>**Из Ленинграда приехала**</u> **/ у вас долго жить будет?**
(Зем 1973:239)
[The woman] from Leningrad, will she stay with you for a long time?

<u>**Булочки продает**</u> **/ перестала к нам ходить//**
(Зем 1973:439)
The person who sells buns stopped coming to our place.

<u>**Окно в коридоре разбил**</u> **/ в вашем классе учится?**
(Зем 1987:55)
Does the person who broke the window in the corridor study in your class?

<u>**С детской коляской**</u> **/ не проходила?**
(Зем 1973:240)
Did the woman with the baby buggy go by?

<u>**Напротив живет**</u> **/ выходит замуж //**
(Зем 1973:239)
[The woman] who lives opposite is getting married.

<u>**Над нами живут**</u> **/ в Киев переезжают //**
(Зем 1973:239)
The people who live above us are moving to Kiev.

Арбузы продает / у него лицо грузинского типа //
(Зем 1981:35)
The guy who sells watermelons has a Georgian face.

Examples as objects:

Не видели / с детской коляской?
(Зем 1973:240)
Have you by chance seen [a person] with a baby buggy?

Я встретил в кино из нашего старого дома //
(Зем 1973:236)
At the movie I met [someone] from our old building.

На балконе сохнет / сними пожалуйста //
(Зем 1973:439)
Please take down that thing drying on the balcony.

Вы не видели / напротив живет?
(Зем 1973:239)
Have you seen [the person] who lives across the way?

Location phrases identifying someone in public can also be used as a form of address:

В середине! Постеснитесь немножко!
(Зем 1973:237)
You in the middle! Squeeze in a little!

У окна! Потише разговаривайте.
(Зем 1973:237)
You by the window! Keep it down.

На задней площадке / проходите пожалуйста вперед // (Лап 1976:354)
You in the back, come forward please.

Pronouns, Adverbial and Noun Phrases That Replace Nouns

A phrase with a logical or specific meaning can substitute for a noun, especially when the verb is present.

Subject:

У тебя нет чем туфли чистить?
(Зем 1987:57)
Would you have something to clean shoes?

У нас где замораживать / маленькая //
(Зем 1971:18)
Our refrigerator has a small freezing compartment.

У вас есть от кашли?
(Зем 1973:227)
Do you have something for a cough?

У тебя не будет / куда яблоки положить?
(Зем 1973:231)
Would you have something to put apples in?

Ботинки чистить / где лежит?
(Зем 1971:19)
Where's that thing to clean shoes with?

Object:

Поставь из чего пить //
(Зем 1973:439)
Set up something to drink from.

Дай чем вытереться //
(Зем 1973:439)
Give me something to wipe with.

Не забудь <u>чем писать</u> //
(Зем 1987:56)
Don't forget something to write with.

<u>Вино открыть</u> / попроси у соседа //
(Зем 1971:19)
Ask the neighbors for a corkscrew.

Возьми <u>на чем сидеть</u> //
(Зем 1973:228)
Grab something to sit on.

Noun and Verb replaced by *который* (which/who/that)

Это какой Толстой? Который «Война и мир"?
(Зем 1987:58)
Which Tolstoy is that? The one who wrote *War and Peace*?

A: А ведь Алиса Порет его ученица //
B: Алиса которая «Винни-Пух»?
(Зем 1987:59)
A. After all, Alisa Poret is one of his students.
B. The Alisa who [did] *Winnie the Pooh*?

A: У моей подруги бронхит //
B: Это какая подруга? Которая на Кировской?
(Зем 1987:59)
A. My friend has bronchitis.
B. What friend? The one who lives on Kirovskaya street?

А которое в бутылках / оно сегодяшнее?
(Лап РЯЗР 1-1968)
That [stuff] in the bottles, is it today's?

А вот эта которая / на ней была кофта / она тонкая?
(Лап РЯЗР 3-1976)
That girl who was wearing a light jacket, is she thin?

IDIOMS, SAYINGS AND PROVERBS

Idioms, sayings and proverbs are certainly a part of Russian vocabulary. They are, however, used in both KLJ and CR and, thus, are not a uniquely integral constituent of the CR system. Therefore, the use of an idiom, saying or proverb does not define CR. For the most part, they fall into the category of items that must be memorized. Perhaps the best book on Russian idioms is Elena Minakova-Boblest's *Modern Russian Idioms in Use*.

SUMMARY OF COLLOQUIAL VOCABULARY

Colloquial vocabulary can be very daunting for the student, since there is no apparent limit to its range. A special challenge to the student is comprehending an utterance where a noun is replaced by a nomination phrase. A dictionary won't help in those instances.

CHAPTER 9

Recommendations

GENERAL

In the last years there has developed an increased interest in CR in the classroom. D. Agatstein, S. Wood and L. Pacira have written articles on the subject. J. Sladkevich reports that CR is the focus of an entire course at her Gdansk University in Poland. O. Solyanik proposes teaching the basics of CR to foreign students at his technical university in Moscow. Additionally, there have been several textbooks that are titled "Colloquial Russian." Unfortunately, as pointed out above, too many of these texts feature what they call 'idioms' and 'colloquialisms.' For example, Wood writes that students should "understand the semantics of Colloquial Russian such as idioms, proverbial Russian and slang."[125]

The above chapters have been aimed at pointing out the importance of CR for Russian language programs and illustrating its systematic nature in the face of its many significant contrasts with KLJ. How then should we proceed to incorporate features of CR into the classroom? Individual teachers and textbook writers will have different objectives and will use their own creativity to do this. Teachers' decisions would be the most appropriate for the classroom. They may find individual aspects of colloquial phenomena more useful than others. This chapter offers some ideas, however, of how CR may be introduced.

First of all, we recommend that when dealing with CR, we call it 'conversational Russian.' Likewise, we should abandon the term 'colloquialism.' This would eliminate some misconceptions about what CR is.

In preparing to incorporate CR into the classroom we must realize certain rather obvious 'facts of life' about any Russian language program. Among them are:

1) All students of Russian should, of course, first learn the formal KLJ version of the language;
2) Consequently, during the elementary stages of the learning process, those elements of CR that do get presented should not distract or confuse the beginner from learning the formal version; and
3) The overriding objective of incorporating elements of CR into the classroom should be to help the student UNDERSTAND, not necessarily produce those elements. Zemskaya makes that point regarding pronunciation:

> … one should take into account that the foreign student need not try to pronounce things in a colloquial way. This would likely lead to him or her not being understood and their speech might sound unnatural and comical. (Зем 87:194)

But knowledge or familiarity of what happens in normal conversational Russian will go a long way to prepare the student to understand CR when he or she encounters it. Ultimately, if the student has the opportunity to visit or live in Russia, a knowledge of CR will allow him or her to operate as comfortably as possible in the native environment.

As regards CR itself, the student is at a cultural disadvantage. We must, consequently, admit further realities:

1) Whether CR is encountered in the spoken or written form, the student is unlikely always to have the situational context at his or her disposal. In the written form, the student will likewise not be able to determine intonation; and
2) If language labs include native speakers who use normal conversational speech (which several audio peripheries to the textbooks referred to above do), phonetic peculiarities of CR will become quickly apparent. Likewise, if the student encounters actual Russian texts (radio scripts, advertisements, newspaper items, etc.), the first difficulties for him or her will probably occur in pronunciation, word order and vocabulary.

In all the categories of the language, however—phonetics, morphology, syntax, word order and vocabulary—there are elements of CR that can be introduced quite early without hindering the overall goal. As the student becomes more competent in the language, the possibilities of introducing more complicated CR elements become more widespread. (Recommended examples are given in bold.)

PHONETICS

Students need not bother with learning all the patterns of vowel and consonant reduction/deletion shown in the Phonetics chapter. In fact, that would be counter-productive and the students could quickly become confused. The examples produced in that chapter are intended only to show they are systematic.

When a student listens to a native or near-native speaker who is speaking at normal conversational speed, he or she soon sees that certain words such as patronymics, numbers and some common words and phrases are pronounced differently in conversation than in KLJ. This could present a learning opportunity where the teacher explains what is going on.

The student should be taught very quickly, however, the rules governing the unstressed *О, Е* and *Я*. This is important for both the formal KLJ and CR. Many words that are introduced at the elementary level provide excellent examples of these unstressed vowels:

> some days of the week (**понедельник, среда, воскресенье**),
> months of the year (**январь, февраль, сентябрь, декабрь**),
> classroom expressions (**повторите, продолжайте, смотрите**).

Whenever practicable, the words provided by Zemskaya in the Phonetics chapter above (and others found in this Zemskaya source) should be introduced.[126]

The [Ъ] is particularly important for both KLJ and CR. Such common words as *голова, хорошо, молоко* use it in both KLJ and CR. Using it correctly will prevent our students from saying, for example, [*Дас] *свиданья*, rather than the correct [дъс] *свиданья*.

MORPHOLOGY

The morphology of CR will present little difficulty for the student. Partitive genitives and colloquial plurals of some nouns can easily be explained. Such examples as **честно** and **по-честному** are easily understood and assimilated. Pronouns don't change form, except for case and number. In CR thcy are used much the same way as in colloquial English. Once all the standard KLJ cases have been covered, it would be useful to say a few words about the vocative.

SYNTAX AND WORD ORDER

These two categories are closely related. For the most part, the patterns in CR syntax should serve only as a basis for comprehension. Nonetheless, the deletion of **быть** from the phrase **может быть** should be easy to cover in early stages of the learning process. The same goes for the substitution of **что** for **почему**.

The deletion of some verbs, connectors and pronouns also might be covered in elementary classes. This occurs in some modern textbooks. Verb deletion examples might be on the order of:

Завтра я в театр.
Куда на каникулы?
Это вы про свою Олю?
Об этом я потом.

Simple pronoun examples could be introduced because they are similar to usage in colloquial English:

Мы вон те возьмем.
Ты эти наденешь?

The deletion in CR of some connectors/conjunctions should not be too difficult, since the same phenomenon occurs in colloquial English as seen in these examples:

А где эта книжка я вчера принес.
Вымой вазу на шкафу.
Жалко девчонки уезжают.

The same applies to reduplication in CR, since it is also similar to colloquial English—that is, it's usually for clarification or emphasis.

Replacing oblique cases with the nominative is a perfect example of why familiarization and comprehension should be the only objects of study in the classroom. We wouldn't want our students to attempt to replicate this phenomenon.

When dealing with word order, comprehension not production once again should also be the primary goal. Grammar is very important here; it is often critical for deciphering word order. The analysis of word order usually can come only after the students have learned the rudiments of Russian grammar. This means it can be dealt with only in the later intermediate or advanced study of Russian.

A logical step in this analysis process might be to reconfigure CR utterances into KLJ sentences. One might start by studying the above examples and why they are translated the way they are into English. There is an additional wealth of examples that could be taken from the many Russian volumes used as sources for this book.

For the advanced student the book *Русская разговорная речь: тексты* (RRRT-78) provides the most complex examples of recorded CR, some of it in phonetic transcription, some in normal orthography. J. Cradler and M. Launer provide an excellent approach to this analysis.[127] They show step-by-step how to reconstruct an example dialogue found in RRRT-78.[128] First, they convert the phonetic transcription to KLJ orthography. Next they show how the all-important, probable situational context can be gleaned from grammatical and word tip-offs in the dialogue. They then show how some referents and the 'deleted' words can be recovered. As pointed out above, thorough knowledge of grammar is paramount here.

Some CR word order will present little problem for the student. Such utterances as:

Команды никакой не было.
Оградку они мне сделали замечательную.
Она слона вчера видела из Индии.
Очень у нее несчастный вид.
Она милая очень женщина

should be easy to translate into KLJ sentences. Later more complex utterances could be introduced. For example:

Твоего брата висит на вешалке плащ.
Мы сейчас с тобой в одну игру будем интересную играть.
Ручку магазин открылся недавно я купил.
Моего сына первая жена ему рассказывали, что докторскую защитила.

VOCABULARY

Unfortunately, the best way to learn vocabulary is to memorize it, either separately or in context. Exercises in word building (словообразование) can also be useful. If Krysin's *Толковый словарь* is available, the student could check to see if any of the basic vocabulary items in his or her lesson have colloquial usages. Students should be cautioned, however, on what they find in standard dictionaries (See the discussion of this in the opening to the Vocabulary chapter). Although particles need to be memorized like other vocabulary items, referral to Vasilyeva's *Particles in Colloquial Russian* would be helpful.

Although they are used infrequently, household terms such as *чайник, кастрюля, солонка* and *плита* should be introduced as early as possible. The same goes for introductory words and phrases. The Russian words **нормально, нормальный** are used so often in contemporary Russian, they should be brought to students' attention early:

Как твоя голова? Не болит?
Нормально.

Как живешь?
Нормально.

Хорошее здесь дно?
Нормальное, песчаное.

The real challenge of CR vocabulary comes with the substitution of phrases where a KLJ word would be used, what is called nomination. At the intermediate and advanced levels descriptive phrases such as **С зелеными балконами /**

это ваш? Молоко разносит / не приходила еще? Не видели / с детской коляской? might be introduced. When pronouns and prepositional phrases replace nouns, this can reinforce the learning of verb governance:

Поставь из чего пить.
Дай чем вытереться.
Не забудь чем писать.

APPENDIX

Source Abbreviations

A-LM	A-LM Russian: Level One
Dawson	Dawson, Bidwell and Humesky
DLIWC	Defense Language Institute, West Coast
Harper	Harper, Koulaeff and Gisetti
Бар	Г.А. Баринова
Вин	Т.Г. Винокур
Горш	А. Горшков
ГрамРЯ	*Грамматика русского языка*
Зем	Е.А. Земская
Иванч	Е. Иванчикова
Кит	М. Китайгородская
Клочк	Э. А. Клочкова
Коз/Гус	Н.А. Козельцева/О.В. Гусева
Кост	В.Г. Костомаров
Крас	Е.В. Красильникова
Крив	А. Кривоносов
Крыс	Л.П. Крысин
Лап	О.А. Лаптева
Лев	В. Левин
Марк/Виш	Ю. Марков / Т. Вишнякова
Некрас	В. Некрасов
Пан	М.В. Панов

Пат/Сан/Кур	З.С. Патралова / З.С. Санджи-Горяева / В.Ф. Курило
Рейм	Л. Рейманкова
Роз	Д. Розенталь.
РЯЗР	*Русский язык за рубежом*
РЯСО	Русский язык и советское общества
Сир	О.Б. Сиротинина
ТолкСлов	Толковый словарь (Krysin)
Швед	Н.Ю. Шведова
Шир	Е.Н. Ширяев
Убог	Ю. Убогий
Улух	Х. Улуханов
Фом	В. Фоменко
Хрест	*Хрестоматия по древнерусской литературе*

ENDNOTES

Abbreviations

SEEJ	*Slavic and East European Journal*
ВЯ	*Вопросы языкознания*
ЛГ	*Литературная газета*
НМ	*Новый мир*
РР	*Русская речь*
РРР	*Русская разговорная речь*
РЯЗР	*Русский язык за рубежом*
РЯНШ	*Русский язык в национальной школе*
РЯСО	*Русский язык и советское общество*
РЯШ	*Русский язык в школе*

AUTHOR'S NOTE

1 I was unaware at the time of Boyanus and Jopson's *Spoken Russian* (1952), a remarkable textbook in that it presents a good picture of the phonetics and intonation of the spoken language. In general, however, it is a text of KLJ and not a treatment of the peculiarities of CR. KLJ is also the primary focus of Mark Sieff's *Colloquial Russian* (1948). There have been several works published on the colloquial speech of other languages. Although not pertaining specifically to Russian, they are noteworthy here since they are repeatedly referred to by Soviet/Russian scholars and show that colloquial speech shares many of the same characteristics, at least, of most Indo-European languages. The views and definitions of colloquial speech given by the various writers are evidence of the fact that these typological and problematic parallels between colloquial and standard written styles of most modern languages suggest the probability that we are talking about universals of colloquial speech. I.B. Hofmann writes of German: "Colloquial speech, first of all expressive speech, is the opposite of the more or less intellectualized written language." For L. Spitzer, Italian colloquial speech "is simply the oral speech of 'correct' (normal, average) speaking Italians."

Ph. Martinon writes: "One does not speak completely as one writes, and the pat phrase 'you speak like a book' is a compliment only in the mouths of the illiterate." Those quotes are in I.B. Hofmann, *Lateinische Umgangssprache*, Heidelberg, 1951; L. Spitzer, *Italienische Umgangssprache*, Bonn-Leipzig, 1922; Ph. Martinon, *Comment on parle en Français*, Paris, 1927. Other works include: Ch. Bally, *Le Langage et la vie*, Geneva, 1952, *Traité de stylistique Français*, Paris, 1951; H. Frei, *La grammaire des fautes*, Paris, 1929; H. Wunderlich, *Unsere Umgangssprache in der Eigenart zur Ihrer Satzfügung*, Weimar-Berlin, 1894; A. Braue, *Beitrage zur Satzgestaltung der Spanischen Umgangssprache*, Hamburg, 1931. All above works cited by Н.Ю. Шведова, *60:*5.

2 My copy of RRR-70 was autographed by Zemskaya, Shiryaev, Krasilnikova, Barinova and Kapanadze.

3 There is a *New Yorker* cartoon where two men are conversing at a cocktail party. The one says, "I understood each and every word you said but not the order in which they appeared." William Haefeli, August 2, 1999.

4 Bold is also used for emphasis and to denote headings.

CHAPTER 1: WHY DID SHE SAY THAT?

5 Костомаров 1965:15.

6 Cited by Овсиенко, «Словарь наиболее употребительных слов русской разговорной речи» РЯЗР 1-67:93. The problems encountered by foreign language students when placed in the native environment are by no means peculiar to Russian. The shock of having studied a foreign language for years and then not being able to communicate effectively in the foreign country is one that is shared by students of many languages. Ken Stanford describes the plight of a young soldier who had just arrived in Germany and was traveling on a train: "He tried to strike up a conversation with one of the other passengers, eager to use his German skills, but was shaken when he couldn't understand a single syllable the man said. It didn't sound like the German he had so diligently studied. He regretted having told the officer in charge of getting him to his assigned base that he wouldn't need any help…he knew German." *The Baker Roaches,* Writer's Republic L.L.C. Union City, New Jersey, 2021:9.

7 Harper, Koulaeff and Gisetti 1966:viii.

8 Isotov SEEJ XII (1968):239-40.

9 Hingley 1959: v, vi. This passage is cited also by Dennis Ward as a footnote in *The Russian Language Today* (Chicago: University of Chicago Press, 1965, p 23.) There are many nuances to the study of CR vocabulary. Given the purpose of this book, we will concentrate only on those general features and patterns of CR vocabulary that may appear often in CR. Detailed illustration of every nuance in CR vocabulary would be overwhelming and intimidating to the student. For those interested in more details about vocabulary in CR, Krysin's dictionary presents additional information. In fact, such an effort is unnecessary in order to introduce general CR vocabulary features into the classroom.

10 Крысин 2008:110-118. Also available on the website Philology.ru, Russian Philological Portal.

11 V. Nekrasov, «Кира Георгиевна» in Harper, Koulaeff and Gisettii 1966:109-110. The next two citations are from this same story on p. 94.

12 For example: «Да что вы загадки-то говорите»? in Ф.М. Достоевский, *Идиот*, 60:81. In most cases, *чего* might be interpreted as short for *отчего*, but the word *почему* seems to be substitutable in the widest range of environments where *что* and *чего* are found.

13 It's interesting to note that this text is sometimes viewed negatively because of its frequent use of colloquial elements. For example, N. Maltsoff's review included the following: "occasionally somewhat too informal or colloquial." (Unpublished in-house review, USMA, West Point, June 1964.).

14 The use of this *может* expression is not unique to Soviet literature. Cf. *– Может, скучно? – прибавил третий.* and *– Я подожду. Может он к вечеру будет*?—two examples found in Dostoevsky's *Idiot*, 1960:431, 662.

15 Абрамов, ЛГ, 7 June 1972.

CHAPTER 2: DEFINITIONS AND SOURCES

16 Such incorrect views on CR even carried over to some Russian language textbooks. In what appears to be an attempt to include CR in its materials, for example, *Ultimate Russian (Advanced)* contains a section labeled *Идиоматика* that contains many phrases, sayings, proverbs and expressions that are neither idioms nor examples of CR. Although idioms form a part of the vocabulary used in CR, they are used also in KLJ and, thus, do not define CR. An idiom is an expression that cannot be understood from the meanings of its separate words, or as Minakova-Boblest in her *Modern Russian Idioms in Use* (2020) states idioms are "a lexicalized reproducible word-group the meaning of which cannot be derived from the meanings of the constituents."

17 Химик, В. "Russian Colloquial Speech: Its Concept, Teaching and Terminology" Международнаяфилологическая конференция, 2014.

18 Webster's New International Dictionary of the English Language, 1935:526.

19 Земская RRR-70:9; RRR-73:17. RRR-73 is a collective work involving several authors. For example, Л.А. Капанадзе, Г.А. Баринова, Е.В. Красильникова and Е.Н. Ширяев made substantive contributions in the book. We cite them when their sections are clearly labeled; otherwise, we cite Земская as the primary editor of the book.

20 Шведова 1960:6-7.

21 Лаптева 1976:65-66. Panov in the series РЯСО uses the term 'style' for anything derived from CR. The term 'style' often will be found with reference to CR in work that was done earlier.

22 Земская RRR-73:17-25. It is interesting to note that at the time, there was considerable disagreement within the Academy on the position taken by Zemskaya and some of her colleagues.

23 Земская RRR-73:19. By 2014, as you will shortly see, she had upgraded *разновидность* to *язык*.

24 Bogdanova-Beglarian points out the complexity of CR when she writes: "Anyone who makes the effort to listen to contemporary Russian everyday speech will certainly be amazed by its clearly specific character. Close examination shows its deviations from the standard language norms… a *different* organization of discourse, *different* units and *different* rules for their functioning—essentially a *different* lexicon and a *different* grammar." (Italics Bogdanova-Beglarian)

25 Земская RRR-87:12.

26 Земская, *Язык как деятельность*, 2014:313.

27 Панов РЯСО *Морфология - синтаксис* 1968:234. РЯСО is a four-volume set dealing with the Russian language as a whole and changes that have occurred over time. There are seven main topics: 1-Principles of the sociological study of the Russian language of the Soviet epoch; 2-Lexicon; 3-Word formation; 4-Morphology; 5-Syntax; 6-Phonetic and 7-Dialects. It is also a collective work, that is, many scholars were involved in its writing. Their names and the topics on which they contributed are listed at the beginning of each volume. All in all, 29 authors made contributions either by writing on a topic or making recordings. Furthermore, there are three pages of names of people and organizations who helped put the series together. M.V. Panov is the overall editor, so we use his name, together with the specific volume when listing sources.

28 Lapteva argues that "There is no spoken form of KLJ." (Cited by Zemskaya 81:58)

29 The following journals were searched: *SEEJ*, *Modern Language Journal* (MLJ) (including a list of all doctoral dissertations since 1958—see *MLJ*, Vols. 44, 47,48, 49, 51, 52, 53, 55 and *SEEJ* Vol.17 (Summer 1973)). Other journals included: *Language*, *Language Learning*, *Russian Language Journal*, *Word* and *Oxford Slavonic Papers*. A computer search made for me by what was then Xerox University Microfilms, DATRIX, Inc. also yielded negative results. Although some work may have been overlooked, the fact that there were few if any references to works in English suggests there were no publications on the subject. Although much of this historical information is not germane to the study of CR in the classroom, we've included it as a fascinating backdrop for teachers and scholars.

30 Шведова 1960:4-7.

31 Шведова 1960:25.

32 Т.Г. Винокур 1968:16. In a footnote on the same page, Vinokur cites O.B. Sirotinina, who writes "Stylized colloquial speech in the works of good writers reflects almost exactly the peculiarities of live speech, based on the study of five kilometers of recorded speech." О. Б. Сиротинина, «Порядок слов живой разговорной речи», *Вопросы синтаксиса и стилистики литературного языка*, Куйбышев: 1963:132.

33 Журавлев 1970:184.

34 Земская 1973:34.

35 Земская 1973:7.

36 Земская 1973:34.

37 Земская 1973:8.

38 Земская 1973:11. Special note: Very many of the references and examples in this book come from the publications of Zemskaya and Lapteva. Although many scholars made substantial contributions to the study of CR, probably all CR scholars will agree Zemskaya and Lapteva were the preeminent experts on the subject. Doctor of Philological Sciences Elena Andreyevna Zemskaya passed away in 2012. Doctor of Philological Sciences Olga Alekseyevna Lapteva passed away in 2020.

CHAPTER 3: BRIEF HISTORY

39 All translations of Gorshkov's citations are mine.

40 И.И. Срезневский, *Мысли об истории русского языка*, 1959. This work was originally written in 1849. Cited by Горшков 1*969*:32.

41 Cited by Улуханов, DLIWC 1972:95. A more complete account of this event can be found in S.A. Zenkovsky 1963:75-76.

42 Cited by Горшков, 1969:113.

43 Cited by Левин, 1972:33.

44 А.С. Пушкин, «Опровержение на критики» (1830). Cited by Горшков 1969:329.

45 Пушкин, «Письмо к издателю» (1836). Cited by Горшков Ibid:330. It's interesting that some 250 years later Земskaya (1987:17) writes of the negative characterization in the utterance "He speaks like he writes." She illustrates this with the following: **Он человек ужасный / говорит книжным языком / даже картошку картофелем называет** // This example is used also in the text above. It's repeated here to show the link with what Pushkin wrote.

46 G.O. Vinokur 1971:127.

47 В Белинский, «О критике и литературных мнениях 'московского наблюдателя'». Cited by Горшков 1969:361.

48 А.Н. Боголюбов, «Об изучении литературных языков: методический очерк», Часть неофициальная, 1914: 9. Cited by Шведова 1960:4.

49 Л.П. Якубинский, «О диалогической речи», в сборнике *Русская речь*», 1923:145. Cited by Шведова 1960:4.

50 See for example А. Селищев, *Язык революционной России* (Москва, 1928); Г. Винокура, *Культура речи* (Москва, 1929); Л. Щерба, «Современный русский литературный язык», *РЯШ* 4-1939; Л. Боровой, «Новые слова», *Красная новь*, 1938-40; С. Ожегов, «Основные черты развития русского языка в современную эпоху», *Известия Академии наук: Серия языка и литературы*, 1951. All works here are cited by A. and T. Фесенко, *Русский язык при советах*, New York, 1955:2.

51 Виноградов *ВЯ* 1-1955.

52 Щерба 1957:116. Cited by Иванчикова, *РЯНШ* 4-1965:13.

53 Т.Г. Винокур, «О некоторых синтаксических особенностях диалогической речи в современном русском языке», 1953. It appeared in a revised version in *Исследования по грамматике русского литературного языка.* Москва: Изд-во АН СССР, 1955.

54 For example, Шведова *ВЯ* 2-56.

55 Шмелев *РЯНШ* 6-1959.

56 Панов *ВЯ* 3-1962.

57 Костомаров *РЯНШ* 1-1965.

58 Костомаров *РЯНШ* 6-1966.

59 Лаптева *ВЯ* 1-1967. This is a wide-ranging review article containing much bibliographic material.

60 Ширяев *РЯЗР* 4-1968.

61 Васильева *РЯЗР* 3-1968, 1-1969, 3-1969. See also a very interesting article in which a Soviet film track (*Друг мой, Колька*) was analyzed for 'kernel' vs. 'derived' structures, frequency of various grammatical forms and vocabulary (Рейманкова, *РЯЗР* 1:1968)

62 In the series РЯСО, edited by Panov, CR was still treated as a style.

63 Крысин *Толковый словарь русской разговорной речи 2014-2021.*

64 Харченко 2016. *Антология русской разговорной речи* (Volume 1: Аграмматизмы – Креация; Volume 2: Литота – Перцепция; Volume 3: Повтор – Словотворчество; Volume 4: Соматизмы – Юмор; Volume 5: Монологи и Постскриптум).

CHAPTER 4: PHONETICS

65 Щерба, *Фонетика французского языка i*n Л.Л. Буланин, *Фонетика современного русского языка*, 1970:98. All the citations from Щерба in the paragraph are found in Буланин.
66 Cited by Буланин 1970:98.
67 Cited by Буланин 1970:55.
68 Аванесов 1954:15-20.
69 Ibid.
70 Панов 1963.
71 Аванесов, Op. cit. 4
72 My son Yasha overheard "данчо" from a Russian on a train in Germany. From the context, he determined it was for 'да ничего'. Although it's true that Russians around the world use many of the same elements highlighted in this book, non-residents of Russia might be influenced by their new environment. Therefore, we've used only authentic examples that were observed in Russia itself.
73 Practically speaking, even 'neutral' phonetic forms present difficulties for students of Russian, since too often they learn 'full' pronunciation and often do not properly reduce [Я, Е, О] in post-tonic or second pre-tonic positions in KLJ words from their textbook lessons. For a discussion of Russian phonetics based primarily on 'neutral' pronunciation, see Л.Л. Буланин.
74 Transcriptions by various authors may differ. This can be explained by the fact that there is often a wide variety of pronunciations and transcription is somewhat subjective.
75 Виноградов ВЯ 1-1955.
76 The book by Boyanus and Jopson—*Spoken Russian: A Practical Course*—is perhaps, even today, the most comprehensive treatment of Russian, including a short history of the language. Its subtitle correctly represents its contents: Written and Spoken Colloquial Russian with Pronunciation, Intonation, Grammar, English Translation and Vocabulary. This work occurred before CR became an objective item for research. Consequently, other than the pronunciation and intonation portions of the book, it deals primarily with KLJ.
77 Брызгунова 1963.
78 Шустикова 1970:47-55.
79 Баринова, «Фонетика,» РРР 73:95.
80 Т.М. Николаева, «О существующих принципах отбора речевого материала при изучении интонации»; Ю. Ванников и С. Абдалян, «Экспериментальное исследование членения разговорной речи на дискретные интонационно-смысловые единицы фразы»; Т.В. Шустикова. «К вопросу об интонации русской разговорной речи»; Г.Г. Полущук, «Роль интонации в дифференциации омонимичных языковых единиц». All in RRR-70.
81 Панов 1963:7.

CHAPTER 5: MORPHOLOGY

82 Земская 1983:80.
83 Красильникова 1970:119-125.
84 Розенталь 1968:99-102, 112-116.
85 Панов, РЯСО *Морфология-синтаксис* 1968:182.
86 Панов, Ibid:175-214; Розенталь 1968:99-102, 112-116.

87 According to Розенталь (1968:112-113), A. Vostokov listed 70 such words in 1831; Chernyshev listed 150 in 1915; a French linguist listed about 200 in 1913.

88 Панов, РЯСО *Морфология-синтаксис* 1968:203-204

89 Панов, Ibid: 68:204. Panov reports a comprehensive statistical analysis of this phenomenon, both by age and profession on pages 205-213. Note the use of **A** in such words as *глаз --глаза* (where **A** is the only acceptable plural) and in words such as *пропуск – пропуски, пропуск – пропуска* (where the **A** versus **И** signifies a different meaning) and has nothing to do with CR.

90 Even Bulgarian, which does not use many of the cases used in Russian, has a vocative. Belorussian considers the vocative "obsolete." See R.G.A. deBray, *Guide to East Slavic Languages*, 1969,1980.

91 Note that the Church Slavonic words are also forms of address.

92 Земская 1987:86

93 Земская 1983:117.

94 Панов, РЯСО *Словообразование* 1968:22.

95 Many scholars have dealt with colloquial word formation, for example Панов, РЯСО *Словообразование* (1968) and Charles Townsend, *Russian Word Formation (1968*). Both Panov and Townsend treat in great detail word formation, but do so for the overall Russian language. Panov does, however, devote Chapter 9 to 'stylistics,' which in essence covers most of the suffixation in CR. A discussion of suffixation takes place by Патралова, Санди-Горяева and Курило in PPP:70:107. Земская devotes chapter IV to suffixation in RRR-87:110-134.

96 Mark T. Hooker 2006:vi.

97 Земская 1973:411

98 Ibid.

99 These and others can be found in Volume I, *Грамматика Академии наук*, 1960:264-271.

100 Патралова, З.С., З.С. Санджи-Горяева, В.Ф. Курило, «Суффиксальное образование существительных в разговорной речи», RRR-70:113.

CHAPTER 6: SYNTAX

101 Early interest in CR by Shcherba, Bogolyubov, Yakubinsky and Vinogradov has already been noted.

102 A. Pereltsvaig provides a long and complex analysis of phrase relocation, which she calls "Split phrases" in *Studia Linguistica,* 2008-1:5.38. Available at worldcat.org/ ILL/AE/mX3sfJuo8.

103 Ширяев, «Связи свободного соединения между предикативными конструкциями в разговорной речи», PPP-70:163.

104 Margaret Mills 1990, in her "Perceived Stress and Utterance Organization in Colloquial Russian," treats with great detail the importance of stress and intonation in words and utterances. Jan Eames Schallert uses the ИК descriptions of Bryzgunova to show how rising and falling utterance contours can work to add to meaning. See Schallert in Mills: 51-65.

105 See also Kurt Woolhiser, "Missing Prepositions in Colloquial Russian Relative Clauses," in Mills:17-29.

106 The назывная функция of the nominative case provides the referential meaning of a word only. See O. Ахманова, *Словарь лингвистических терминов*, 1966:247. The Academy Dictionary refers only to a *назывное* предложение. Ozhegov does not list the word *назывной*.

WORD ORDER

[No notes for this chapter. All sources are given in parentheses.]

CHAPTER 7: VOCABULARY

107 Michelle Berdy provides some examples of current neologisms that are based on English. Among them are some that are useful for conversation today in Russia: *нетворкинг* – networking; *кроссовки* – running shoes, as opposed to *кеды* – sneakers, and *баскетки* – basketball shoes. Two words that may bring a smile to an English speaker are the words for 'like' and 'hate,' as in these two examples: *Текст набирает высокий рейтинг, юзеры лайкают его* – The text is gaining a high rating; users get a lot of 'likes'; *Почему люди начинают хейтить то, что стало популярным?* – How come people are starting to hate something that has become popular? Michelle Berdy, "Survival Russian," *Russia Life* magazine, May-June 2020, p. 26. The word *лайкать* appears in Krysin's *Толковый словарь...*, Vol. 2, p. 176 with the note that it is a computer term. The dictionary gives several examples of its use in CR. The word *хейтить* may be in Volume 5—not yet published.

108 Девкин 1973:441. Cited in footnote by Земская, *Русская разговорная речь: лингвистический анализ и проблемы обучения*, 1987:27.

109 Денисов/Костомаров 1970:69-75

110 So far as colloquial vocabulary is concerned, this problem has now been somewhat ameliorated by the newly published *Толковый словарь русской разговорной речи*, which we discuss at the end of this chapter.

111 Dictionaries have some interesting data that relate indirectly to colloquial speech and, more importantly, to the language overall. See Mark T. Hooker's Chapter 8: "Dictionaries as History," in which he shows how dictionaries reflect changes in Russian as a result of the demise of the USSR and Communist influence. In particular, see his presentation on the terms 'capitalism' and 'capitalist.' Hooker 2006:125-131.

112 *2380 наиболее употребительных слов русской разговорной речи*, Москва, Изд-во Университета Дружбы Народов им. Патриса Лумумбы, 1968.

113 Vakar 1964:1

114 Vakar 1964:1-8 See Josselson, *The Russian Word Count*. Detroit: Wayne University Press, 1953. Штейнфельдт, *Частотный словарь современного русского литературного языка*. Таллин, 1963.

115 Vakar's reviewer, J. Paternost, wrote that his work "certainly reflects the actual usage of spoken (literary) Russian more fully and more accurately than any other list prepared in or outside the Soviet Union. It is astonishing that in a conversation with the author of the A-LM second edition, it was discovered that she had not known of the existence of РЯНШ until it published a favorable review of her book. Apparently, the intensive discussion of CR in that journal in 1965-1966 went unnoticed in this country."

116 Марков/Вишнякова РЯНШ 6-1965.

117 Василенко/Кольцова 1970:82-88.

118 Земская 1987:33fn.

119 Крысин, *Толковый словарь русской разговорной речи*. Москва: Изд-во Дом ЯСК. Выпуск 1 (А-И), 2014, 550 copies; Выпуск 2 (К-О), 2017, 300 copies; Выпуск 3 (П-Р), 2020, 300 copies; Выпуск 4 (С-Т), 2021, 300 copies. A fifth volume has yet to be published.

120 This entry and the *что-то* entry are not found in the dictionary, but it are provided in Krysin's 2008 article, «Некоторые принципы…" The *что-то* entry may appear in Volume 5 of the dictionary.

121 Козельцева and Гусева (1970:114) write that for every 1000 words they found in their live, recorded corpus, there were 135 particles in dialogue and 100 in monologue. The most frequent particles are *НУ* and *ВОТ*. Zemskaya (Зем 1983:94), citing N.A. Prokurovsky, states the percentage of particles in scientific Russian is 1.6; in CR 12.6.

122 One might view as a deficiency the fact that many of Vasilyeva's examples are taken from written literature, whereas most other examples used in this book are from live, recorded colloquial speech. Use of Vasilyeva's examples, however, are appropriate because they are found also in live CR and she provides the best explanations. Furthermore, as we have stated above, our students may have their first contact with CR in Russian literature. Some of her English translations have been altered. The examples provided here are found on pages 46-169.

123 An example not given by Vasilyeva, but one that is quite common in CR is *Да нет*! (Oh no!) It's used by Kozeltseva and Guseva in RRR-70:116 – **Вот уж и сессия. –Да нет, я просто так**, and Vasilenko and Koltsova in RRR-70:83 **–Там больница напротив. – Да нет, ну вот с угла на угол, красное здание.** Cf. **– Разве сюда втекает Средиземное море? – Да нет. Сюда идет Красное море от Великого, или Тихого океана…** (В. Аксенов, «Перемена образа жизни» in Harper et al), 1966:55.

124 Michelle Berdy 2020:28. For a detailed treatment of the importance of context, see P.G. Finedore 1990, in Mills 1990:175-186. Zemskaya (2014: 414) writes that in normal conversation the "connection between verbal and non-verbal factors is quite important."

CHAPTER 8: RECOMMENDATIONS

125 Sarah Wood, "Colloquial Russian Within the Classroom."

126 Another example of possible confusion is distinguishing between Russian *двенадцать* (12) and *девятнадцать* (19). Sometimes it's a matter of counting the syllables. *Двенадцать* has three syllables, while *девятнадцать* has four. Despite a correct explanation of the reduced vowels, one textbook (*Colloquial Russian: the Complete Course for Beginners)* teaches incorrectly on page 46 that *ee* (her) is pronounced (ye-yo). That is not the case in KLJ or CR.

127 J. Cradler and M. Launer in Mills 1990: 187-196.

128 RRRT:31-32. The requirements and procedures used in providing the examples in RRR-78, as well as the informant information, are the same as described above in this book, taken from RRR-73. RRRT is a collective work authored by Баринова, Земская, Капанадзе, Красильникова and Ширяев.

SOURCE BIBLIOGRAPHY

Abbreviations

SEEJ	*Slavic and East European Journal*
RLJ	*Russian Language Journal*
ВЯ	*Вопросы языкознания*
ЛГ	*Литературная газета*
НМ	*Новый мир*
РРР	*Русская разговорная речь*
РЯЗР	*Русский язык за рубежом*
РЯНШ	*Русский язык в национальной школе*
РЯСО	*Русский язык и советское общество*
РЯШ	*Русский язык в школе*

SOURCES IN THE LATIN ALPHABET

Agatstein, David. "Colloquial Russian in the Classroom," RLJ XLII, Nos. 141-143, 1988.

A-LM Russian: Level One. New York: Harcourt, Brace & World, Inc., 1963.

Baldwin, John R. *A Formal Analysis of the Intonation of Modern Colloquial Russian*. Hamburg: Helmut Buske Verlag, 1979.

Berdy, M. "Survival Russian," *Russia Life* magazine, May-June 2020.

Blanchei, Jack. *Ultimate Russian (Advanced).* New York: Living Language, Random House, 1968.

Boyanus, S.C. and N.B. Jopson. *Spoken Russian: A Practical Course.* London: Sidgwick and Jackson, LTD, 1952.

Cradler, James F. and Michael K. Launer, "Teaching Aural Comprehension of Colloquial Russian," in Mills, *1990.*

________________________________ "Teaching Aural Comprehension of Colloquial Russian," RLJ XLII, 1988.

Dawson, C.L., C.E. Bidwell and A. Humesky, *Modern Russian I.* New York: Harcourt, Brace & World, Inc., 1964.

DLIWC (Defense Language Institute, West Coast), «Слово устное и слово письменное», Reference Pamphlet, Vol. XI-7.

Ervin, Gerard L., Sophia Lubensky, Larry McClellan and Donald K. Jarvis. *Начало, Book Two.* Boston: McGraw Hill, 2000.

Goodman, Paula Finedore, "Context, Cohesion and Colloquial Russian," in Mills, 1990.

Harper, K., G. Kourlaeff and M. Gisetti, Eds. *New Voices: Contemporary Soviet Short Stories.* New York: Harcourt, Brace & World, Inc., 1966.

Harrison, William, Yelena Clarkson and Stephen Fleming. *Colloquial Russian.* London: Routledge & Kegan Paul, 1978.

Hingley, R. ed. *Soviet Prose.* New York: Pitman, 1959.

Hooker, Mark T. *Implied, But Not Stated: Condensation in Colloquial Russian.* Llyfrawr, 2006.

Isotov, N. Review of "Kira Georgievna" by V. Nekrasov. SEEJ XII (1968).

Khavronina, S. *Russian As We Speak It.* Russky Yazyk Publishers. Moscow: 1968.

Le Fleming, Svetlana and Susan E. Kay. *Colloquial Russian: The Complete Course for Beginners.* Fourth Edition. London and New York: Routledge, 2017.

Mills, Margaret. A Multiaspectual Analysis of Word Order in Colloquial Russian. PhD Dissertation, University of Michigan, 1985.

____________ Ed., *Topics in Colloquial Russian.* New York: Peter Lang Publishing, Corporation, 1990.

Minakova-Boblest, Elena. *Modern Russian Idioms in Use*. Moscow-Munich: Azbuka, 2020.

Pacira, L. "Toward an Approach to Teaching Russian Conversational Courses," RLJ XL No. 140 (Fall 1987).

Paternost, J. Review of *A Word Count of Spoken Russian* by N. Vakar, SEEJ XI (1967).

Nummikoski, Marita. *Troika.* New York: John Wiley and Sons, Inc., 1996.

Rosengrant, Sandra Freels. *Russian in Use.* New Haven and London: Yale University Press, 2007.

Pereltsvaig, Asya. "Split Phrases in Colloquial Russian" in *Studia Linguistica*, Vol. 62-1, 2008 (wordcat.org/ILL/AE/mX3sfjuo8).

Schallert, J.E. "Intonation Beyond the Utterance: A Distributional Analysis of Rising and Falling Contours," in Mills, 1990.

Shlyakhov, Vladimir and Eve Adler. *Russian Slang & Colloquial Expressions*. 2nd Edition. New York: Barron's Educational Series, Inc., 1999.

Sieff, Mark. *Colloquial Russian*. London: Routledge & Kegan Paul Limited, 1948.

Sobolov, Olga, Natasha Bershadski, Svetlana le Fleming and Susan E. Kay. *Colloquial Russian 2: The Next Step in Language Learning*. London:Routledge, 2019.

Townsend, Charles. *Russian Word Formation*. New York: McGraw-Hill Book Company, 1968.

Vakar, N. *A Word Count of Spoken Russian*. Columbus: Ohio State University Press, 1966.

Vasilyeva, A.N. *Particles in Colloquial Russian*. Moscow: Progress Publishers, 1972.

Vinokur, G. *The Russian Language:History*. Translated by M.A. and J. Forsyth. Cambridge: University Press, 1971.

Unbegauen, B. "Colloquial and Literary Russian," *Oxford Slavonic Papers*, I (1950).

Wood, S. "Colloquial Russian Within the Classroom," filelibsnu.at.ua.

Woolhiser, C. "'Missing Prepositions in Colloquial Russian Relative Clauses," in Mills, 1990.

Zenkovsky, S.A. Ed., *Medieval Russian Epics, Chronicles and Tales*. New York: E.P. Dutton, 1963.

SOURCES IN THE CYRILLIC ALPHABET

(Some entries are duplicated: author, title, editor)

2380 наиболее употребительных слов русской разговорной речи. Москва: Изд-во Университета Дружбы народов им. Патриса Лумумбы, 1968.

Абрамов, Ф. «Какие нужны словари»? ЛГ, 7 июня 1972.

Аванесов, Р. *Русское литературное произношение*. Москва: Учпедгиз, 1954.

_____________*Русское литературное произношение*. Издание 4-е, переработанное и дополненное. Москва: Просвещение, 1968.

В. Аксенов. «Перемена образа жизни» *in New Voices: Contemporary Soviet Short Stories*. New York: Harcourt Brace Jovanovich, Inc., 1966.

Ахманова, О. *Словарь лингвистических терминов*. Москва: Советская энциклопедия, 1966.

Баринова, Г.А. Фонетика, Глава II in РРР-73.

Bogdanova-Beglarian, N. «Устная спонтанная речь и разнообразие происходящих в ней процессов», *Contemporary Issues of Linguistics and Translation*, Issue III, Saint Petersburg State University, November 2016 (cyberleninka.ru).

Брызгунова, Е. *Практическая фонетика и интонация русского языка.* Москва: Изд-во Московского университета, 1963.

_____________«Интонация и смысл предложения», РЯЗР 1-1967.

_____________«Основные типы интонационных конструкций и их употребление в русском языке», РЯЗР 1-1973.

_____________«Основные типы интонационных конструкций и их функцирование в русском языке», РЯЗР 2-1973.

Бубнис, В. «Три дня в августе», НМ 2-1974.

Будагов, Р. *Литературные языки и языковые стили.* Москва: Высшая школа, 1967.

Буланин, Л. *Фонетика современного русского языка.* Москва: Высшая школа, 1970.

Василенко, Т.А., Т.И Кольцова, «Некоторые лексические особенности разговорной речи», РРР-70.

Васильева, А. «Глагол в разговорной речи: императив», РЯЗР 1-1969.

_____________ «Глагол в разговорной речи: индикатив», РЯЗР 3-1969.

_____________ «Глагол в разговорной речи: инфинитив», РЯЗР 3-1968.

_____________ «Разговорная речь как функциональный стиль», *Вопросы стилистики в преподавании русского языка иностранцам.* Москва: 1972.

Виноградов, В. «Итоги обсуждения вопросов стилистики», ВЯ 1-1955.

Винокур, Т. «О некоторых синтаксических особенностях диалогической речи», *Исследования по грамматике современного русского языка.* Москва: Изд-во АН СССР, 1955.

____________ «К характеристике понятия разговорной речи», РЯНШ 2-1965.

____________«Некоторые особенности стилистической системы русского языка», РЯНШ 4-1966.

____________«Об изучении функциональных стилей русского языка советской эпохи», *Развитие функциональных стилей современного русского языка.* Москва: Наука, 1968.

____________ «Стилистическое развитие современной русской разговорной речи», *Развитие функциональных стилей современного русского языка.* Москва: Наука, 1968.

Вишнякова, Т. «О некоторых проблемах обучения разговорной речи», РЯНШ 3-1965.

_______________«Некоторые особенности употребления полных прилагательных в разговорной речи», РЯНШ 1-1967.

_______________«Некоторые статистические характеристики имен существительных и прилагательных: из анализа живой разговорной речи», РЯНШ 2-1967.

Горшков, А. *История русского литературного языка*. Москва: Высшая школа, 1969.

Грамматика русского языка 1-2. Издание 2-е. Под редакции В.В. Виноградова. Москва: Изд-во АН СССР, 1960.

Денисов, П.Н., В.Г. Костомаров, «Стилистическая дифференциация лексики и проблемы разговорной речи», РРР-70.

Достоевский, Ф. *Идиот*. Москва: Государственное изд-во художественной литературы, 1960.

Журавлев, А.П. «О некоторых отличиях живой русской разговорной речи от стилизованной», РРР-70.

Земская, Е.А. «О понятии разговорная речь», *Русская разговорная речь*. Саратов: Изд-Во Саратовского университета, 1970.

__________«Русская разговорная речь». ВЯ 5-1971.

__________*Русская разговорная речь: лингвистический анализ и проблемы обучения*. Москва: Русский язык, 1987.

__________Ответ. редактор, *Русская разговорная речь: фонетика, морфология, лексика, жест*. Москва: Наука, 1983.

__________ Ответ. редактор, *Русская разговорная речь*. Москва: Изд-во Наука, 1973.

__________*Язык как деятельность:морфема, слово, речь*. Москва: Изд-во ФЛИНТА, Изд-во Наука, 2014.

Иванчикова, Е. «Синтаксические приметы разговорной речи всовременной публицистике», РЯНШ 4-1965.

Китайгородская, М. «О случаях нарушения управления в разговорной речи», РЯШ 3-1973.

Кожевникова, К. «О функциональных стилях», РЯНШ 2-1968.

________________и О. Кафкова. «Лингвистическая и педагогическая проблематика разговорного стиля», *РЯНШ* 2-1966.

Клочкова, Э.А. «О влиянии формы разговорной речи на распределение классов слов», РРР-70.

Козельцева, Н.А., О.В. Гусева, «Незнаменательная лексика разговорной речи», РРР-70.

Костомаров, В. «Разговорная речь: определение и роль в преподавании», РЯНШ 1-1965.

_____________ «К итогам дискуссии о разговорной речи», РЯНШ 6-1966.

_____________*Русский язык на газетной полосе*. Москва: Изд-во Московского университета, 1971.

Красильникова, Е. «Конструкции с удвоением в русской разговорной речи», РЯШ 5-1971.

Кривоносов, А. «Гори, гори ясно», НМ 3-1974.

_____________ «Простая вода», НМ 11-1970.

Крысин, Л.П. «Некоторые принципы словарного описания разговорной речи (Постановка задачи)», *Русский язык в научном освещении,* №2 2008 (16). Also on the website philology.ru.

_____________«Лексикографическое представление разговорной речи в толковом словаре», РЯЗР 4-2016.

_____________Ред., *Толковый словарь русской разговорной речи*. Москва: Изд-во Дом ЯСК. Выпуск 1 (А-И), 2014; Выпуск 2 (К-О), 2017; Выпуск 3 (П-Р), 2020; Выпуск 4 (С-Т), 2021.

Лаптева, О. «О структурных компонентах разговорной речи», РЯНШ 5-1965.

_____________«О некодифицированных сферах современного русского языка», ВЯ 2-1966.

_____________«Изучение разговорной речи в отечественном языкознании последних лет», ВЯ 1-1967.

_____________«К вопросу о месте современной устно-разговорной речи в кругу явлений литературного языка», РЯЗР 1-1968.

_____________«Литературная и диалектная разновидности устно-разговорного синтаксиса и перспективы их сопоставительного изучения», ВЯ 1-1969.

_____________ *Русский разговорный синтаксис*. Москва: Изд-во «Наука», 1976.

Левин, В. «Петр 1 и русский язык». *Известия Академии наук: серия языка и литературы*», 3-1972.

Лексические минимумы русского языка. Москва: Изд-во Московского университета, 1972.

Марков, Ю, Т. Вишнякова, «Русская разговорная речь: 1200 наиболее употребительных слов», РЯНШ 6-1965.

Некрасов, В. «Кира Георгиевна» in *New Voices: Contemporary Soviet Short Stories*. New York: Harcourt Brace Jovanovich, Inc., 1966.

Овсиенко, Ю.Г. «Словарь наиболее употребительных слов русской разговорной речи», РЯЗР 1-67.

Панов, М. «О развитии русского языка в советском обществе», ВЯ 3-1962.

__________ «О стилях произношения», *Развитие современного русского языка.* Москва, 1963.

__________«О литературном языке», РЯНШ 1-1972.

__________Ред., *Русский язык и советское общество. 1- Принципы социологического изучения русского языка советской эпохи. 2-Лексика. 3- Словообразование. 4- Морфология. 5-Синтаксис. 6-Фонетика. 7-Народные говоры.* Москва: «Наука», 1968.

Патралова, З.С., З.С Санджи-Горяева, В.Ф. Курило, «Суффиксальное образование существительных в разговорной речи», РРР-70.

Рейманкова, Л. «Материалы к изучению русской разговорной речи», РЯЗР 1-1968.

Розенталь, Д. *Практическая стилистика русского языка, Издание 2-е, исправленное и дополненная.* Москва: Высшая школа, 1968.

Русская разговорная речь. Ред. О. Сиротининой. Саратов: Изд-во Саратовского университета, 1970.

Русская разговорная речь. Ред. Е. Земской. Москва: Наука, 1973.

Русский язык и советское общество. Москва: Изд-во «Наука» 1968.

Сиротинина, О.Б. Ред., *Русская разговорная речь.* Изд-во Саратовскогоуниверситета, 1970.

____________ О.Б., И.С. Кузмичева, Л.И. Сирченко, Л.Т. Токарева, Н.И. Травкина, «Некоторые синтаксические особенности разговорной речи», РРР-70.

Сладкевич, Жанна. «Обучение разговорной речи на уроках русского как иностранного», *Балтийский акцент*, 4-2013, worldcat.org/ILL/
AE/8L1sfJuo8.

«Слово устное и слово письменное», DLIWC Reference Pamphlet, Vol. XI-7.

Соляник, О.Е. «Преподавание основ разговорной речи иностранным учащимся технического ВУЗа», *Приволжский научный вестник*, Московский технический университет им. Н. Баумана, (cyberleninka.ru), 2015.

Толковый словарь русской разговорной речи. Москва: Изд-во Дом ЯСК, 2014-2021.

Убогий, Ю. «На новом месте», ЛГ, 24 апреля 1974.

Улуханов, Х. DLIWC 1972:95.

Фесенко, А. и Т. Фесенко. *Русский язык при советах.* New York: 1955.

Фоменко, В. «Память земли», НМ 11-1970.

Харченко, В.К. *Антология разговорной речи: Некоторые аспекты Теории.* Volume 1: *Аграмматизмы – Креация*; Volume 2: *Литота – Перцепция*; Volume 3: *Повтор – Словотворчество*; Volume 4: *Соматизмы – Юмор*; Volume 5: *Монологи и Постскриптум*. Москва: Изд-во URSS, 2016.

Хасанов, Н. «Использование образцов разговорной речи», РЯНШ 4-1966.

Химик, В. "Russian Colloquial Speech: Its Concept, Teaching and Terminology" (in Russian), Международная филологическая конференция, Петербургский государственный университет, 2014.

Хрестоматия по древнерусской литературе. Москва: Высшая школа, 1969.

Шанский, Н. *Фразеология современного русского языка.* Москва: Высшая школа, 1969.

Шведова, Н. «К изучению русской разговорной речи: реплики-повторы», ВЯ 2-1956.

____________*Очерки по синтаксису русской разговорной речи.* Москва: Изд-во АН СССР, 1960.

____________ «О некоторых активных процессах в современном русском синтаксисе», ВЯ 2-1964.

Ширяев, Е. «Реплики диалога как предложения», РЯШ 6-1966.

____________ «Модели предложения с нулевыми полнозначными глаголы-предикатами», РЯЗР 4-1968.

____________ «Связи свободного соединения между предикативными конструкциями в разговорной речи», PPP-70.

Шмелев, Д. «О некоторых особенностях употребления вопросительных местоимений и наречий в разговорной речи», *РЯНШ* 6-1959

Шустикова, Т.В. «К вопросу об интонации русской разговорной речи» PPP-70.

ACKNOWLEDGEMENTS

In addition to all the Soviet/Russian scholars who provided much of the material and analysis for this book, I am indebted to the following individuals who were instrumental in my putting this book together.

Svetlana Morozova of the Eastview Publications office in Moscow, who acquired for me several books on Colloquial Russian that were not otherwise available.

Kenneth McKenzie, the Interlibrary Loan Librarian at Colorado State University, Pueblo, who provided many valuable works that were available at various locations in the U.S.

Mark T. Hooker and James Cradler, who read an early manuscript and made important comments on it, many of which were incorporated into the final version.

Mistakes in the final version, of course, are mine.

Printed in the United States
by Baker & Taylor Publisher Services